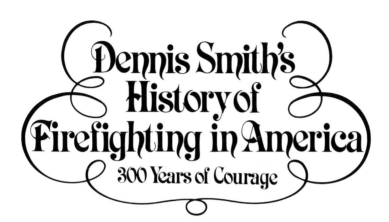

Dennis Smith's
History of
Firefighting in America
300 Years of Courage

BOOKS BY DENNIS SMITH

Report from Engine Co. 82
The Final Fire
Firehouse
Dennis Smith's History of Firefighting in America

Dennis Smith's History of Firefighting in America

300 Years of Courage

THE DIAL PRESS

NEW YORK

32055

Published by
The Dial Press
1 Dag Hammarskjold Plaza
New York, New York 10017

Photograph and illustration credits:
Jacket photograph by John E. Bowen courtesy *Firehouse Magazine,* 515 Madison Avenue, New York, N.Y. 10022.
Photo Research: Helena Frost
P. 1, Brown Brothers. 2, Culver Pictures. 3, Illinois Historical Society. 4 (left), Picture Collection, New York Public Library (N.Y.P.L.); (right), Insurance Company of North America (I.N.A.). 5, Colonial Williamsburg Foundation. 6, Smithsonian Institution. 10, I.N.A. 12, Picture Collection, N.Y.P.L. 14, Smithsonian Institution. 16, Brown Brothers. 17, I.N.A. 18 (top and bottom left), Brown Brothers; (bottom center and right), Culver Pictures. 19 (top left and right, center, bottom), Culver Pictures; (top center), Wide World. 21, Culver Pictures. 22, Brown Brothers. 25, The Historic New Orleans Collection. 27, Culver Pictures. 28, 29, I.N.A. 30 (top), Culver Pictures; (bottom), I.N.A. 31 (top left, right and bottom left), I.N.A. 33, 34, Culver Pictures. 35, I.N.A. 36 (top), Culver Pictures; (bottom), I.N.A. 37, Picture Collection, N.Y.P.L. 38, Brown Brothers. 39, 40, I.N.A. 41, Culver Pictures. 42, Wells Fargo Bank History Room. 44, 45, Culver Pictures. 48, Carnegie Library of Pittsburgh. 49, Picture Collection, N.Y.P.L. 50, Missouri Historical Society. 53, 59, Culver Pictures. 60 (left), I.N.A.; (center), Collection of Mrs. Joseph Carson; (right), The Historic New Orleans Collection. 61 (top), Culver Pictures; (bottom), Picture Collection, N.Y.P.L. 62, 66, Culver Pictures. 69, Museum of the City of New York. 70, 78, Culver Pictures. 81, 84, Picture Collection, N.Y.P.L. 85, 87, Courtesy of Bostonian Society/Old State House. 89, Picture Collection, N.Y.P.L. 90, Culver Pictures. 91, I.N.A. 92, Picture Collection, N.Y.P.L. 93, Culver Pictures. 94, Missouri Historical Society. 95, 97, Picture Collection, N.Y.P.L. 98, Culver Pictures. 99 (top left), Picture Collection, N.Y.P.L.; (right), The Historic New Orleans Collection; (bottom left), Picture Collection, N.Y.P.L. 101, Denver Public Library, Western History Department. 102, 104, Culver Pictures. 105, 107, Picture Collection, N.Y.P.L. 108 (top), Brown Brothers; (bottom), Culver Pictures. 110, 112, Culver Pictures. 113, U.P.I. 115, 116, Brown Brothers. 119, Culver Pictures. 120, The Historic New Orleans Collection. 121, 123, Brown Brothers. 125, 126 (top), Picture Collection, N.Y.P.L. 126 (bottom), Culver Pictures. 127, U.P.I. 128, Culver Pictures. 129, U.P.I. 130, 131, Brown Brothers. 132, Picture Collection N.Y.P.L. 133, 135, U.P.I. 136, Wide World Photos. 138, 139 (top), U.P.I. 139 (bottom), Wide World Photos. 140, 142, 143, 145, U.P.I. 146, 148, Wide World Photos. 149 (top and bottom), U.P.I. 150, Wide World Photos. 151, U.P.I. 152, 155, 156, Wide World Photos. 158, U.P.I. 159, Documentary Photo Aids. 160, Wide World Photos. 162, 163, U.P.I. 164 (top), Wide World Photos; (bottom), New York Fire Department. 165, Wide World Photos. 166, New York Fire Department. 167, U.P.I. 168, New York Fire Department. 169, Wide World Photos. 170, New York Fire Department. 172 (top), Brown Brothers; (bottom left), Wide World Photos; (bottom right), New York Fire Department. 173, Wide World Photos. 174 (top), New York Fire Department; (bottom), Wide World Photos. 175, New York Fire Department.

Special thanks to the following people for their assistance in the preparation of this collection of illustrations and photographs: Debra Force, Curator, I.N.A. Museum; Tome Logan, Culver Pictures; Mr. & Mrs. Collins, Brown Brothers; Arthur Corr, Photo Unit, New York Fire Department.

Manufactured in the United States of America

First printing

Library of Congress Cataloging in Publication Data

Dennis Smith, 1940–
    Dennis Smith's History of firefighting in America.

    Includes index.
    1. Fire prevention—United States—History.
    2. Fire departments—United States—History. 3. Fires—United States—History. I. Title. II. Title: History of firefighting in America.
TH9503.S53   363.3'7'0973   78–15128
ISBN: 0–8037–2538–8

To the wives and children of today's firefighters,
who give so much

ACKNOWLEDGMENT

A book such as this does not come together through the efforts of a single individual, but rather, as in firefighting, the job gets done because of the hard, enthusiastic, and dedicated work of a team of talented persons. Consequently, I would like to thank my editor, Nancy van Itallie, whose gentle ways and editorial insight make writing more a pleasure than a task.

I would also like to thank Helena Frost, whose gay spirit is matched only by her expertise in finding appropriate artwork in little-known corners, and her husband, Bill, who puts it all together.

Thanks as well to Paul Ditzel for reading the proofs.

And then there are my wife, Patricia, and my children, Brendan, Dennis, Sean, Dierdre, and Aislinn, who make each day more meaningful than the one before.

Finally, and most particularly, there is Janet McHugh, whose grandfather was a Chicago fireman, and whose research, concern, and friendship brought so much to the making of this book—to her my unending affection and gratitude.

D.S.
1978

NOTABLE AMERICAN FIRES

Jamestown, Virginia, 1608
Dutch ship *Tiger,* Manhattan Island, 1613
Plymouth Plantation, Massachusetts, 1623
New Amsterdam, 1628
Boston, Massachusetts, 1631
Boston, Massachusetts, 1653
Boston, Massachusetts, 1676
Boston, Massachusetts, 1679
Boston, Massachusetts, 1711
Philadelphia, Pennsylvania, 1730
Charleston, South Carolina, 1740
New York, New York, 1741
Boston, Massachusetts, 1760
New York, New York, 1776
New Orleans, Louisiana, 1788
New Orleans, Louisiana, 1794
Detroit, Michigan, 1805
Washington, D.C. (during War of 1812)
Savannah, Georgia, 1820
New York, New York, 1835
Pittsburgh, Pennsylvania, 1845
New York, New York, 1845
St. Louis, Missouri, 1849
San Francisco, California, 1849
Philadelphia, Pennsylvania, 1850
San Francisco, California, 1850
San Francisco, California, 1851
Sacramento, California, 1852
Crystal Palace, New York City, 1858
Pemberton Mill, Lawrence, Massachusetts, 1860
New York Tenement Fire, 1860
Charleston, South Carolina, 1861
Draft Riots, New York City, 1863
Atlanta, Georgia, 1864
Savannah, Georgia, 1865
Richmond, Virginia, 1865

Portland, Maine, 1866
Chicago, Illinois, 1871
Peshtigo, Wisconsin Forests, 1871
Boston, Massachusetts, 1872
Brooklyn Theater, Brooklyn, New York, 1876
Seattle, Washington, 1889
Spokane, Washington, 1889
Cripple Creek, Colorado, 1896
Jacksonville, Florida, 1901
Iroquois Theater, Chicago, Illinois, 1903
Baltimore, Maryland, 1904
General Slocum Steamer, New York City, 1904
San Francisco, California, Earthquake, 1906
Lake View Elementary School, Collinwood, Ohio, 1908
Chicago, Illinois Stockyards, 1910
Triangle Shirtwaste Company, New York City, 1911
Black Tom, New Jersey Munitions Depot, 1916
Northern Minnesota Forests, 1918
Cleveland, Ohio, Clinic, 1929
Columbus, Ohio, State Penitentiary, 1930
S.S. *Morro Castle* Cruise Ship, 1934
Cocoanut Grove Nightclub, Boston, Massachusetts, 1942
Ringling Brothers and Barnum & Bailey Circus, Hartford,
    Connecticut, 1944
LaSalle Hotel, Chicago, Illinois, 1946
Winecoff Hotel, Atlanta, Georgia, 1946
Texas City, Texas, 1947
St. Anthony's Hospital, Effingham, Illinois, 1949
Our Lady of the Angels Elementary School, Chicago, Illinois,
    1958
Watts Protest, Los Angeles, California, 1965
23rd Street Fire, New York, New York, 1966
Gulf Oil Refinery, Philadelphia, Pennsylvania, 1975
Beverly Hills Supper Club, Southgate, Kentucky, 1977

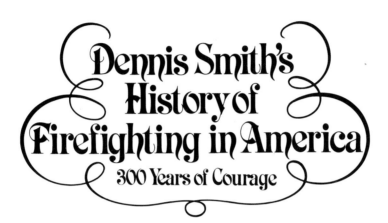

Dennis Smith's History of Firefighting in America

300 Years of Courage

The recorded story of fire in America begins on a spring day in May of 1607 as one hundred strong, determined, optimistic Europeans camped on a flat swampy peninsula on the James River. They named the place Jamestown, and it was here that the settlers found new hope for a free and productive life. But it proved to be a difficult life, and they were ill-equipped to sustain the hardships of a wild, as yet unconquered land. Many died the first winter—of pneumonia, malaria and dysentery. By January of 1608 only thirty-eight settlers had survived, and most of them were racked with disease, and disabled.

Renewed hope swept through the small community with the arrival that month of Captain Christopher Newport and eighty new colonists. With them came the gunpowder, tools, food and beer needed for survival, and the settlers stored the supplies in buildings of rough hewn lumber—the only products of their new adventure.

Hope was short lived however, for within a few days the first recorded fire in America occurred when the com-

Jamestown settlers build cabins of rough-hewn timber.

AMERICA'S FIRST RECORDED FIRE

JAMESTOWN, VIRGINIA
1608

munity blockhouse caught fire. Nearly every building in America's first settlement was destroyed in that first year.

Captain John Smith wrote of the fire in his journal: "Most of our apparel, lodging and private provision were destroyed."

Without their dwellings and supplies the colonists were now fully exposed to a severe winter, and many more of them perished.

It was a great effort to rebuild Jamestown. The colony sank to its lowest ebb in the winter of 1609 when it suffered through what came to be called "the starving time." But the settlement gradually grew and prospered, becoming the capital of the Virginia colony. Out of the ashes of America's first fire grew a spirit to rebuild and to rise to the challenges of adversity that has been the mainstay of the American people throughout their history.

CHIMNEY AND THATCH FIRE

PLYMOUTH
1623

Farther north, in Massachusetts, fire also threatened the lives and settlement of the colonists. Three years after the Pilgrims established Plymouth Plantation in 1620 a visitor described the settlement as having "about twenty houses, four or five of which are fair and pleasant." In November of that year, 1623, fire besieged Plymouth colonists as it had those in Jamestown fourteen years earlier, nearly devastating the young colony.

The thatched roofs of Plymouth houses provided ready fuel for chimney sparks.

According to the governor, William Bradford:

This fire was occasioned by some of the sea-men that were roystering in a house wher it first begane, making a great fire in very could weather, which broke out of the chimney into the thatch, and burnte down 3. or 4. houses, and consumed all the goods and provissions in them. The house in which it began was right against their storehouse, which they had much adoe to save, in which were their commone store and all their provissions; the which if it had been lost, the plantation had been overthrowne.*

Bradford's journal speaks of what was perhaps the chief cause of fire during the early Colonial period—chimneys. In America as in Europe at the time chimneys were made of wood, lined and covered with mortar or mud. As the covering grew dry, it would chip away from the wood, exposing the chimney directly to fire. Even if the chimneys were sound, they often became clogged with wood tar, which would catch fire and throw sparks onto the roofing, usually made of thatch. Thatch naturally provided perfect kindling for the sparks, and any fire would quickly spread to the wooden timbers and plank walls of a structure, as happened at Plymouth.

The Plymouth experience was sadly repeated a few years later. The Puritans came to establish a colony in Boston in 1630, and there they built the same kind of houses as the Plymouth Pilgrims. Within eight months of their arrival, they suffered the same kind of fire.

The Puritans responded to their misfortune, as people would do over and over again throughout the development of American firefighting, by creating laws only after a serious destruction of either life or property had occurred, instead of planning safeguards ahead of time. The Boston selectmen ordered that "noe man shall build his chimny with wood, nor cover his house with thatch." With this decree America's first fire regulation was enacted.

While fire caused setbacks to the efforts of colonization, on one occasion it actually served to encourage settlement. In the early 1600s, following Henry Hudson's exploration of the river named for him, Dutch seamen were already carrying on trade with the Indians of Manhattan Island. In 1613, the Dutch ship *Tiger*, moored near

*There is some evidence that this might indeed be the first case of arson in the New World, for Bradford goes on to raise suspicions about those that "were not friends" who were near the scene of the fire. He also mentions a firebrand found in a nearby shed.

Wood-and-mud chimneys were a common 17th-century fire hazard.

FIRST FIRE REGULATIONS
BOSTON
1630

DUTCH SHIP TIGER
MANHATTAN
1613

the mouth of the Hudson River, caught fire. The fire forced the seamen to stay on Manhattan for the entire winter, giving them time to construct a new ship. During that time they learned of the potential of New York's waterways and of the lushness of its vegetation. On their return to the Netherlands that spring, word quickly spread of the promise of the land where they had stayed. Soon thereafter Dutch trading companies were colonizing New Amsterdam.

The first structures built to house the Dutch settlers were of "board and bark." Here too, thatched roofs were the order of the day. Crowded together at the southern tip of Manhattan Island, these flimsy buildings were easy prey to fast-moving chimney fires, which were frequent and often disastrous.

Firefighting in New Amsterdam, as in all the American colonies, was highly informal, to say the least, and it was completely a volunteer effort. When fire was sighted, the cry of "Throw out your buckets" rang out. Householders would throw out the leather fire buckets they kept at hand, and neighbors and passersby would grab them, dip them into the nearest water available, get as close to the fire as they dared, and throw. Very often the neophyte firefighters produced more pandemonium than efficiency, and buildings burned to the ground.

Peter Stuyvesant, the feisty one-legged governor of New Amsterdam, decided in 1647 that order must be brought to firefighting. In that year, the town passed an ordinance similar to the one that Boston had passed in 1631—wooden chimneys and thatched roofs were strictly forbidden. Also, chimneys had to be swept regularly to keep them clear of dangerous wood tar.

FIRE REGULATIONS

NEW AMSTERDAM
1647

Left: Leather fire bucket, New York City, 1805.

Right: Fire axes—long an important part of firefighters' gear

Teeth were put into these regulations in 1648 with the appointment of four fire wardens. They were empowered to inspect all the chimneys of the community, and to fine any and all offenders, making this America's first fire prevention act.

Householders at the time were fined twenty-five florins if fire occurred in their homes, and these fines were used to buy and maintain ladders to reach fires on roofs, hooks to pull down burning buildings or buildings in the path of a fire, and fire buckets. All of this equipment was to be "in readiness at the corners of streets and in public houses, for time of need." To even better insure fire protection a later ordinance called on citizens to fill three three-gallon buckets of water at sunset and leave them on their doorsteps.

The city burghers also appointed eight volunteers to form a "rattle watch." The most prominent citizens of the colony volunteered for fire duty to set a good example for their less spirited brethren. Nicknamed "The Prowlers," these men patrolled the streets from nine in the evening till dawn. At the first sign of fire they sounded the alarm on the fire rattles they carried, and after gathering the waiting buckets and hooks and ladders they raced to the fire scene. There they directed neighbors and passersby into bucket brigades, with one line passing the filled buckets from the water source to the fire and the other passing the emptied buckets back to be refilled.

Peter Stuyvesant had said that all fire regulations must be met with the least expense and danger to the community, but even minimal protection is better than no protection at all as we shall see.

The fire precautions succeeded in protecting New Amsterdam, and later New York, from a major city fire for nearly a century.

Boston, however, was less fortunate, and over the next two centuries it repeatedly suffered major fires. The first broke out along the waterfront on a frozen January night in 1653. Unlike New Amsterdam, Boston was not prepared. There was no fire watch or system to rouse the people, and no buckets, ladders, hooks, or axes were provided for such an emergency.

As the fire spread, people madly tried to salvage whatever they could from buildings in the path of the fire. Quickly recruited firefighters soaked blankets and attempted to cover roofs with them. Others wet swabs at

FIRE WARDENS

NEW AMSTERDAM
1648

Fire rattle used as alarm by Colonial night patrols

WATERFRONT FIRE

BOSTON
1653

the end of long poles and tried to extinguish sparks as they landed on roofs.

Yet the fire raged on. Hooks and chains were found and used to pull down buildings to make a fire break, but the flames continued to thwart all attempts to stop or control them. Barrels of gunpowder, stored in homes and public houses all over the settlement, began to explode, sending still more embers into the winter air and onto neighboring roofs.

By dawn the fire had burned itself out, but it had taken with it about a third of the town's dwellings and several warehouses full of supplies the townspeople needed.

The next day, of course, the town leaders determined that some safeguards against additional fire destruction must be made and they drew up a list of ordinances somewhat like those in New Amsterdam. Every house was to have a ladder that reached the roof. Every householder was to have a twelve-foot pole "with a good large swob at the end of it." "Iron Crooks, with Chaines" were to be hung on the side of the meeting house, "thear to be redy in Case of fier." Finally, provision was made for "a bellman for to goe about towne in the night" from ten in the evening until five in the morning.

A year later, Boston contracted with Joseph Jynks (often spelled Jenks), an iron maker, for an "Ingine" to carry water to fires. Probably it was a syringe pump supplied by water from a bucket brigade.

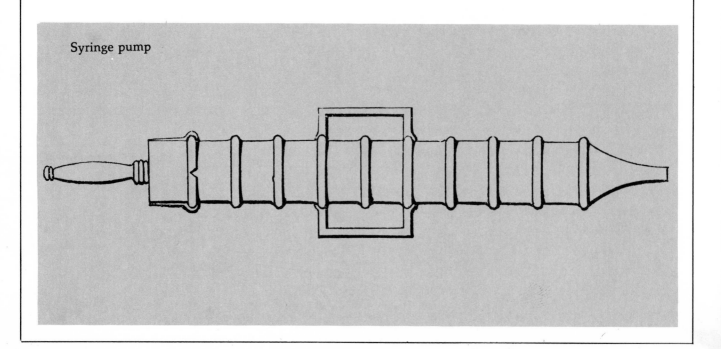

Syringe pump

Boston's new ordinances did not succeed in saving the city from further devastating fires. In November of 1676 the cry of "Fire!" again went up, and in no time the conflagration was out of control and racing through flimsily, closely built structures and leaping across narrow, winding streets. Bucket brigades were simply no match for it. Nor was Joseph Jynks' "Ingine," and for the first time in Boston, gunpowder was used to blow up buildings to create fire breaks. But still the fire raged.

For four hours the fire burned a path through town. Finally providential rains came and drowned the blaze. Fifty dwellings had been destroyed, along with several commercial buildings and a church.

Again Boston leaders met to formulate more ordinances that would be too little and too late. Recognizing the fire hazard posed by the unchecked and unsupervised building of structures along Boston's twisting streets, they issued this prelude to today's building codes:

> Honrd. councill Dec 28 1676. Upon complaint made by the selectmen of Inconveniences of ye straightness of ye streets latelie laid waist by fire, it is ordered that noe person presume to build again without the advise & order of ye selectmen till the next General Court.

It was at this time that the colonists began to suspect that more was responsible for their fires than cruel fate and highly flammable building materials. In the 1670s, incendiaries were at work in many American towns. Boston especially seemed plagued by a determined band of firebugs. Whether or not they were responsible for the fire in 1676 is not known, but they did make repeated attempts to start other fires. Fearful of their actions, the General Court issued this order in October 1677:

> Whereas many secret attempts have been made by evil-minded persons to set fire to the town of Boston and other places tending to the destruction and devastation of the whole; this Court doth account it their duty to use all lawful means to discover such persons, and prevent the like for time to come.

While Bostonians searched for the firebugs in their midst, they also sought to improve their firefighting equipment. Shortly before the great fire of 1676, Boston had ordered a fire engine from London. Actually, the "engine" was a pumper, a tublike wooden box three feet long and eighteen inches wide. It was equipped with car-

EARLY BUILDING CODE

BOSTON

1676

ARSON PREVENTION

BOSTON

1677

FIRST ENGINE COMPANY

BOSTON
1679

rying handles and a direct-force pump from which came a small hose. A bucket brigade was required to keep the tub filled as the hose played water on the fire.

This pumper brought about the establishment of the first engine company in the Colonies and the origin of paid fire departments in America. The General Court hired a reputable and responsible carpenter, Thomas Atkins, to act as captain of twelve men who were to "engage to take care of the manageing of the sd engine" and were to be paid for their work.

It was not long before the new engine company was fighting the work of firebugs. Only four months after the engine arrived from England, it and its crew were put to an impossible test. On an August midnight in 1679, incendiaries succeeded in setting fire to an alehouse called the Sign of the Three Mariners. Located near several warehouses, it served as a perfect starting-off point for a devastating fire.

The new engine company battled the fire with little success. The tide in Boston Harbor had gone out, and water to fight the flames was scarce. After twelve hours the fire finally burned out, but not before eighty dwellings and seventy warehouses lay in ruins.

Two months later, the General Court again tried to forestall future city fires by issuing Boston's first building act:

> The Court having a sense of the great ruin in Boston by fire and hazzard still of the same by reason of joining and nearness of their buildings, for prevention of damages and loss thereby for future. Do therefor order and enact that henceforth no dwelling-house in Boston shall be erected and set up except of stone or brick and covered with slate or Tyle. . . .

The Court also banished several people it suspected of being arsonists and expanded the fire watch. They divided the city into wards and put militia officers in command of firefighting efforts in each district. The new provisions also ordered more publicly owned buckets, hand engines, swabs, axes, and gunpowder, and increased the amount of firefighting equipment that homeowners were obligated to provide.

Still, the Court's efforts were not altogether successful, and Boston would continue to be visited by major fires.

Just two years later in 1682, the Quaker settlement of Philadelphia was being mapped out by its founder, William Penn. Fire was on his mind as he sketched the gridiron pattern of straight, wide streets. Penn's father had been caught in the great fire that had devastated the city of London in 1666, and young Penn himself remembered the narrow, crooked lanes of London with their houses leaning into one another. He knew how fire had galloped through them sixteen years earlier, and Penn was intent on seeing that Philadelphia would not suffer London's fate. His city plan, along with fire regulations passed in 1696, helped to save Philadelphia from a great city fire for the first fifty years of its life.

In 1711, Boston was again struck by a serious fire, and it was one that would have long-range effects on firefighting in America. At about seven o'clock in the evening of October 2, "a poor Scottish woman, named Mary Morse," was picking over some highly combustible oakum. She was working by firelight, and it was not long before the flame made contact with the oakum. The fire was out of control immediately, and owing to the great drought the city was suffering the leaping tongues of heat spread easily and quickly from building to building.

The burning progressed for seven hours, consuming some hundred houses in the most thickly populated and wealthiest section of town, taking with it the post office and the Town House. As it approached the old Meeting House, several heroic seamen attempted to climb its high steeple to save the bell that hung there. But before they reached it the roof fell in, and they and the bell were lost. Several other lives were lost in attempts to blow up other buildings to create desperately needed fire breaks.

This fire, the most devastating suffered in the Colonies to that date, left 110 families homeless. It also left a lasting and far-reaching impression on a six-year-old who witnessed it, Benjamin Franklin, and some of the multitudinous contributions to society he would later make were a direct result of his experiences that October night.

Amid the ruins, Bostonians were again forced to examine their ability to cope with fires, and again they found it lacking. On October 31, the General Court created "An Act providing in case of fire for more speedy extinguishment thereof, and for the preserving of goods

WILLIAM PENN'S CITY PLAN

PHILADELPHIA

1682

OAKUM FIRE

BOSTON

1711

APPOINTMENT OF FIREWARDS

BOSTON

1711

A BLACK SEAMAN

In the early history of firefighting in America, stories of seamen's courage constantly recur. Because of their experience and agility in climbing the rigging of sailing ships, they were invaluable in fighting fires that threatened churches from their steeples. Since the ladders of the time were quite short, only seamen could or dared try to reach these high places.

One seaman who dared was a black sailor in Charleston, South Carolina. His name is lost to us but his act is not. As fire raged through that port city one night, its light fell upon St. Philip's, the tallest and most beautiful church in Charleston. As the flames worked their way toward the surrounding park and cemetery, the minister and the faithful stood guard, armed with buckets and ladders, ready to put out any embers that struck their church's roof or walls. For a while they succeeded in dousing any threatening flames, but then a stray ember landed on the top of the church steeple, seemingly far above anyone's ability to reach. As the faithful looked on helplessly, the church seemed doomed.

Suddenly, through the smoke, the figure of a black sailor appeared on a ladder, heading toward the belfry. Once there, he scaled the steeple, where he ripped away the blazing shingles with his bare hands, tossing them outward so that they would fall harmlessly to the ground. The grateful congregation watched as the sailor singlehandedly saved their church from certain destruction. In appreciation for his courageous act, the people of St. Philip's bought him his freedom and equipped him with his own fishing boat.

Firewards' staffs identified their bearers' office.

endangered thereby." The act not only attempted to find ways to regularize the manner of fighting fires, but also to discourage looting during them. It pointed out that "divers evilminded and wicked persons, on pretence of charitably offering their help" were taking advantage of the confusion during a fire "to rob, plunder, embezzle, convey away and conceal the goods and effects of their distressed neighbours."

The act called for the appointment of "prudent persons of known fidelity" to act as firewards in different sections of town. These worthy citizens were to "have a proper badge assigned to distinguish them in their office, a staff of five feet in length coloured red, and headed with a bright brass spire of six inches long." The act outlined their duties:

> . . . the officers . . . are required upon the notice of fire breaking
> forth, taking their badge with them, immediately to repair to the place,
> and vigorously to exert their authority for the requiring of assistance,
> and using utmost endeavours to extinguish or prevent the spreading
> of the fire and secure the estate of the inhabitants; and due obedience
> is required to be yielded to them and each of them accordingly for that
> service.

Another firefighting innovation to grow out of the Boston fire of 1711 was the Mutual Fire Societies. The General Court's actions in providing firewards and other protections did not much diminish the fears of many Bostonians anxious to protect their goods and property. As a result, groups of twenty or so people banded together with the pledge that should fire strike one of them, all would come to aid. Not only would they help the town firefighters in putting out the fire, but they would also salvage as many belongings as possible and guard them from looters.

Standard equipment for each society member was a salvage bag and a bed key. The salvage bag was roomy enough to hold as many valuables as a man could scoop up before an advancing fire. As beds were often among the most expensive of a colonist's goods, they were among the first things to be saved, and the bed key was used to unscrew the sections of a bed so that it could be removed to safety.

The Mutual Fire Societies became social as well as protective associations, setting a pattern for organized volunteer firefighting groups, which would one day be the backbone of firefighting in America and would dominate it for a century and a half.

Such societies were well established in Boston when Benjamin Franklin, now eighteen years old, left there for Philadelphia. Within a few years of his arrival in the City of Brotherly Love, Philadelphia's fifty-year immunity from a major fire came to an end. In 1730 fire attacked the Fishbourne wharf area, causing considerable damage. Realizing that their fast-growing city needed more and better firefighting equipment, officials ordered two fire engines from England, as well as four hundred leather buckets, twenty ladders, and twenty-five hooks.

Boston-bred Franklin was an avid observer of firefighting measures in his adopted town. As a newspaper publisher there, he advised his readers on taking precautions against fire, and he often commented on Phil-

THE FISHBOURNE WHARF FIRE

PHILADELPHIA
1730

Firemen at work, 1733

FIRST VOLUNTEER COMPANY

PHILADELPHIA
1736

adelphia's firefighting capabilities. In 1736 an extensive fire prompted him to take a still more active role in dealing with fire. He decided to form a fire brigade that would not only race to the burning property of its members (as did the Mutual Fire Societies), but would also respond to any fire calls in their vicinity. When he called for volunteers, thirty prominent, civic-minded citizens clamored to join, and America's first volunteer company—christened the Union Fire Company—was born.

Franklin's idea was such a popular one that more and more volunteers kept presenting themselves. Feeling that no more than thirty or forty men should make up a company, Franklin advised them to form additional companies—the beginning of a Fire Department. The Fellowship Fire Company, the Hand-in-Hand, the Heart-in-Hand, and the Friendship quickly followed the Union Fire Company, and gave Philadelphia a strong firefighting organization.

These volunteer companies provided their equipment at their own expense—engines, ladders, and so on —and stored it at strategic places in the community. At the signal of a fire each man was to respond carrying a salvage bag and fire bucket. On their arrival their chief, or fireward, would direct them in setting up a bucket brigade, pumping the engine, pulling down burning timbers with hooks, or whatever other work needed to be done in fighting the fire.

To the south of Philadelphia in this period, in Charleston, South Carolina, another defense against fire devastation was being developed. Charleston, or Charles Town as it was then called, had been established at about the same time as Philadelphia, and it was experiencing similar prosperity and growth. The need for expansion demanded rapid building, and so hastily and flimsily constructed buildings were placed along ill-planned streets.

Inevitably, fires occurred from time to time—often enough for "a meeting of sundry of the Freeholders of this Town" to offer proposals "for establishing an Insurance office against FIRE." In 1736, they published their Articles of Agreement:

> WHEREAS the Insurance of Houses against Fire hath by experience been found to be of very great service, to many Persons, who would otherwise have been reduced to Poverty and Want. And whereas, by reason of our Distance from Great-Britain, no Insurance Office there, will upon any Terms or Conditions, Insure any House in this Town from Loss by Fire; and it being natural for Men to form themselves into Companies and Societies, in order to guard against those Evils and Mischiefs, which separately and in their distinct capacities they would not be able to avoid. . . .
>
> . . . We do convenant, promise, conclude and agree, That we will, and we do by these Presents form ourselves (as far as by Law we may) into a SOCIETY for the mutual INSURANCE of our respective Messuages and Tenements in Charles Town (which shall be entered in Books of the Directors of the Society to be insured) from Losses by Fire, and do name and call ourselves the FRIENDLY SOCIETY.

This first fire insurance company in the Colonies was probably equipped to cover fire losses of the kind suffered in Charleston up until that time. Unfortunately it was not able to cope with what happened four years after its founding. On November 18, 1740, fire broke out and, fanned by a northwest wind, "consumed the Houses from Broad Street and Church Street down the Granville Bastion, which was the most valuable part of the Town on account of the Buildings and Trade." It continued to burn for six hours, with an estimated loss of three hundred houses, as well as storehouses, stables, and several wharves.

As the ashes smoldered, the city fathers showed unerring hindsight by enacting a fire law that prohibited the use of any materials other than brick or stone in

FIRST FIRE INSURANCE COMPANY
CHARLESTON
1736

construction. But the fire legislation came too late for the Friendly Society. Fire losses wiped the company out of existence. It would be several years before another American venture into fire insurance would succeed. This time it would be under the leadership of the old firehorse Benjamin Franklin.

FOUNDING OF ENGINE COMPANY No. 1

NEW YORK
1731

Meanwhile, New York was continuing to maintain its firefighting standards. In 1731, it had taken delivery of two "enjines from London." They were Newsham pumpers—the finest fire engines constructed up to that time. Unlike the old pumpers that were able to send water out only in spurts, the Newshams could send *"continual streams with great force."* The engines had long levers running along either side that several men would pump up and down. This pumping action both drew water into the gooseneck nozzle and drove it up and outward toward the fire. The engine could be used either by extending a suction hose into a nearby well or reservoir, or supplying water to it by a bucket brigade.

The best way of extinguishing most fires, even today, is to get as close as possible to the fire and pour water on it, and the Newsham pumpers had this great advantage of being small enough to be brought directly into a house, and thus come close to the fire. The maker claimed that they "would go through a passage about three foot wide

Newsham engine

in complete working order, without taking off or putting on anything, and may be worked with ten men in such passage."

Like the Philadelphians, New Yorkers were soon forming volunteer fire companies. The first Newsham pumper caused the founding of New York's Engine Company No. 1, under the direction of a brewer named Peter Rutger. The second became the pride of Engine Company No. 2, under the leadership of two merchant brothers named Roosevelt—John and Nicholas.

But even New York's foresight could not prevent a major fire any longer. Just as Philadelphia's luck had run out in 1730, so New York's ran out in 1741. Actually the growing town was struck not by one, but by a series of fires. The first and most damaging broke out in the governor's house, which was located inside Fort George, at the southern tip of the island. New York's volunteer firemen rushed their two Newshams to the scene, but a gale wind sent the flames racing through the fort, soon consuming everything within its walls.

At first, suspicion about the fire's origin was directed at a plumber who had carelessly left open coals near the governor's house. But after a few smaller fires occurred within the next few days, conspiracy rather than carelessness was suspected—and a racial conspiracy at that.

New York was familiar with racial hatred. Slaves had first been brought there in 1628, and now two thousand blacks lived in the town of ten thousand. White New Yorkers feared a slave uprising, and it was whispered among colonists that the frequent fires were a sign that such an uprising had begun. In their hysteria and readiness to believe lies, New Yorkers were not unlike Salem's residents at the time of the witchcraft trials. Blacks were rounded up virtually indiscriminately, as were whites who were accused of leading them in the "Negro Plot."

Within five months, suspicions about a conspiracy had produced these disastrous results:

> . . . one hundred and fifty-four negroes were committed to prison, fourteen of whom were burnt at the stake, eighteen hanged, seventy-one transported, and the rest pardoned or discharged for the want of sufficient evidence. In the same time, twenty-four whites were committed to prison, four of whom were executed.

The main accuser in the affair was rewarded for her work with one hundred pounds, but soon her lies went

THE "NEGRO PLOT"

NEW YORK
1741

beyond even the most hysterical people's belief. When she began to accuse prominent and powerful New Yorkers, the townspeople seemed to understand that they had been had. In their embarrassment, they chose quietly to forget the matter, again imitating the behavior of Salem's townspeople.

In 1743 New York's City Council decided that it needed to add more engines to protect its growing territory. This time it did not have to look to England. A cooper and boatbuilder who lived in Maiden Lane, Thomas Lote, had developed an American engine that could compete with the British-made Newshams. Unlike the Newsham, its pumping levers were located at the front and back, but the action was equally powerful. New York ordered Lote's machine, and it went to Engine Company No. 3. There its gleaming copper fittings, incongruously, earned it the name "Old Brass Backs."

A few years later, in 1752, Benjamin Franklin made his final major contribution to American fire protection. Having helped to see to it that, through its building regulations and several fire companies, Philadelphia maintained a good fire record, he decided that a fire insurance

THE FIRST AMERICAN PUMPER

NEW YORK
1743

An early pumper

THE GREAT GREEN TREE CONTROVERSY

The firemark of the Mutual Assurance Company, Philadelphia, 1805

In the late eighteenth century Philadelphia was a city of straight, wide, and tree lined streets, a truly idyllic early American community. The trees, though, were a topic of controversy among the city's power brokers for the first five years of the 1780s. It seems that in addition to providing shade on hot summer days, the trees also created obstructions for firefighters in the course of raising ladders, positioning pumpers, and running hose lines. Trees also increased the fire hazard to the houses they fronted, and helped to spread the flames once a fire began.

Consequently, Benjamin Franklin and the Philadelphia Contributionship ordered that no houses fronted by trees were to be insured, and managed not so coincidentally to push through a piece of municipal legislation that called for the removal of all trees from the streets of the City of Brotherly Love. Irate citizens, however, caused this bit of anti-esthetic commercialism to be repealed, and a Dr. Benjamin Rush hastily gathered a group of tree lovers in 1784 to resolve the problem. Rush and his friends decided to insure their own tree-fronted houses, and created the Mutual Assurance Company that would insure all homeowners willing to pay an extra-risk premium for the comforting shade of their street trees.

This early consumer activism served also to end the virtual monopoly that the Philadelphia Contributionship enjoyed in the city until that time.

The symbol chosen for the firemark of the Mutual Assurance Company? A green tree, of course.

17

FAMOUS AMERICANS WHO SERVED AS VOLUNTEER FIREFIGHTERS

George Washington fighting a fire.

Thomas Jefferson

George Washington

Benjamin Franklin

Paul Revere

Samuel Adams

Alexander Hamilton

John Hancock

John Jay

John Barry

Aaron Burr

Benedict Arnold

19

BENJAMIN FRANKLIN'S INSURANCE COMPANY

PHILADELPHIA
1752

THE GREAT FIRE OF 1760

BOSTON
1760

The firemark of the Philadelphia contributorship, 1774

company in his own city would have a much better chance of success than had the one in Charleston. As a consequence he founded the "Philadelphia Contributionship for the Insurance of Houses from Loss by Fire." The "Contributors" were to be "equal Sharers in the Losses as well as the Gains."

The company adopted a firemark that was to identify each policyholder's property. Its design reflected the joint effort involved in the Contributionship and was called the "Hand-in-Hand." This firemark, generally made of wood or metal, was to be attached to the policyholder's property. It showed the fire companies that came to fight a blaze that they should restrain their enthusiastic use of axes and hooks and keep property damage "thro Indiscretion" down to a minimum.

The city of Boston, so often ravaged by great fires that it had to number them by the years in which they happened—the Great Fire of 1653, of 1673, of 1679, of 1711—was devastated by yet another conflagration in 1760. And once again, Boston had the dubious honor of breaking a fire record—for the greatest fire losses suffered to date in the American colonies. The number of buildings destroyed was set at "174 dwelling houses and tenements and 175 ware houses, shops and other buildings with a great part of the furniture besides large quantities of merchandize. That the loss upon moderate computation cannot be less than £100,000 sterling." In today's dollar currency that would be about $1.7 million.

As one eyewitness recounted the scene on March 20:

> . . . it is not easy to describe the terror of that fatal morning, in which the imagination of the most calm and steady received impression that would not easily be effaced. The distressed inhabitants of those buildings wrapped in fire scarce knew where to take refuge: numbers were confined to beds of sickness, as well as the aged and the infant, when removed from house to house, and even the dying were obliged to take one remove more before their final time.

Several prominent citizens who had lost their property in the fire petitioned "the Honble the commons of Great Britain, in Parliament assembled" for desperately needed help. Two years later their plea was acknowledged, but there is no record that any action was taken to comply with their request.

Such callous treatment could not have endeared the British government to the Bostonians, many of whom were growing more and more restive under British rule.

In the years that followed, this restiveness led to rioting and attacks on British tax collectors and customs officials in Boston. To restore order there, the British stationed six hundred troops in the city. Confrontations between the redcoated soldiers and the irate townspeople were common and potentially explosive.

On March 5, 1770, the explosion came. A mob of Bostonians was taunting a British sentry near the Customs House and pelting him with snowballs and chunks of ice. As the mob grew larger and the sentry more frightened, townspeople raced through the streets yelling "Fire," bringing out more people. Church bells rang out, a common Colonial fire alarm, and brought still others into the area, many of them with fire buckets in hand.

Soon the mob near the Customs House had grown greatly in number and brazenness. The sentry had now been joined by six or seven other soldiers, and the tight little group tried to back away from the menacing crowd. Then a club flew out of the mob and struck one of the redcoats. Staggered by the blow, he shouted, "Damn you, fire!" He fired and so did the others, killing five men and wounding several more.

The stunned crowd finally dispersed, carrying off the dead and wounded. Soon the colonies were abuzz with talk of the "Boston Massacre," and anti-British sentiment grew. Blood had been spilled between British and Ameri-

THE BOSTON MASSACRE
BOSTON
1770

The Boston Massacre, 1770

Lower Manhattan burning, 1776

cans for the first time. It would not be the last. Within five years, there would be open revolt.

As in all wars, fire was used as a weapon in the American Revolution. More than once the British used it to threaten and demoralize the citizenry. For example, shortly before the Battle of Bunker Hill in 1775, they set fire to four hundred dwellings in Charlestown, across the river from Boston. This move was calculated not only to divert the attention of the American patriots preparing to defend Boston, but also to break the will of the angry rebels.

The Americans are strongly suspected of having used fire on at least one occasion to leave nothing behind but desolation for the approaching British troops. It happened in New York City in 1776, after General George Washington and his weary army had been defeated at the Battle of Long Island. Retreating to the hills of upper Manhattan Island, Washington looked back on the city and saw hundreds of structures that would provide comfortable winter quarters for the oncoming British soldiers. Knowing that the British "would derive great convenience" from a city left standing and knowing that two thirds of it was owned by British loyalists, Washington

Left: Engine panel from a Philadelphia fire company
established in 1796 shows Washington at the battle
of Trenton. (Insurance Company of North America)

Top: An early engine panel from a fire company in New
Jersey depicting "Glory." (Insurance Company of North America)

Above: Early jumper-type hose reel. (Culver Pictures)

Below: Mutual Assurance Company
fire mark, 1784; Insurance Company
of North America's first fire mark, 1794.

Right: Benjamin Franklin, firefighter
(top), and Philadelphia-style engine
model, 1842 (bottom).

(Insurance Company of North America)

Below: Parade hats from two nineteenth-century fire companies.

Bottom: Engine panel depicts "Rescue" as two firemen arrive to help woman from upper-story room.

Right: Early decorative engine panel from Philadelphia.

Lower Right: Fire mark of the Philadelphia Contributorship, 1753.

(Insurance Company of North America)

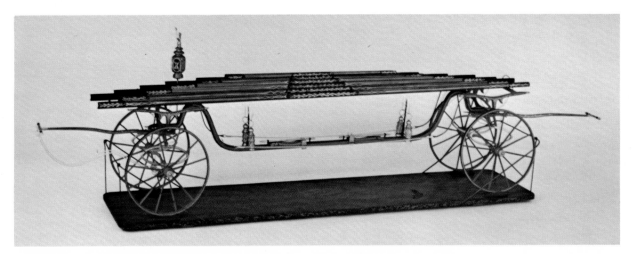

Above: Washington Company hand-drawn hook-and-ladder model, New Jersey, 1816.

Left: Membership certificate of the Friendship Fire Company of Baltimore, 1850s. Note firefighting tools on borders.

(Insurance Company of North America)

wrote the Continental Congress asking whether to destroy New York or not.

The Congress considered Washington's questions, and after some deliberation they decided against using this "scorched earth" tactic. But the Congress did not reckon on the actions of the people in New York who were not loyal to the British. Five days after Washington departed, mysterious fires broke out in lower Manhattan. Gale winds from the southwest sent the fires racing over a large area. British troops scrambled to man the engines and buckets and to press civilians into fighting the fire. But the engines broke down, the buckets had been slashed, and many civilians were anything but cooperative. Adding to the British woes, a fire alarm could not be sounded because the church bells had been carried away to be turned into American cannon.

Dawn of September 21 broke on an angry British command that now had five hundred fewer dwellings in which to quarter its army. General Washington took a happier view: "Providence, or some good honest fellow, has done more for us than we were disposed to do for ourselves."

During the Revolutionary War, firefighters were generally considered exempt from military service, since they were so sorely needed in their communities. Nevertheless many of them joined up, eager to fight an enemy other than fire. Members of one company in particular, the Hibernia Fire Company of Philadelphia, went in numbers and served with distinction.

Several of these Hibernians founded and fought in Philadelphia's Fire Cavalry Troop, "one of the most distinguished for its service and good conduct of any engaged in the revolutionary struggle." When General George Washington discharged the troop from duty after the war, he extended to them "his most sincere thanks for the many essential services they have rendered to their country, and to himself personally during the course of that severe campaign." He added, "Though composed of gentlemen of fortune, they have shown a noble example of discipline and subordination, and in several actions, have shown a spirit and bravery, which will ever do honor to them, and will ever be gratefully remembered by me."

The war duty of several of the Hibernia Company men was not limited to active service. Several of them contributed heavily to finance the war effort, an "essen-

REVOLUTIONARY FIRE TACTICS
NEW YORK
1776

tial service" that led to the financial ruin of at least three of them.

With the end of the Revolution, firefighters who had gone to war—and had come through it safely— returned to their homes and cities in the newly independent United States. There they joined their old companies or formed the new ones needed by their growing communities.

THE GREAT FIRE OF NEW ORLEANS

NEW ORLEANS
1788

The last great fire of the 1700s happened far to the west of the rapidly developing eastern cities in a burgeoning settlement with a vastly different background and legacy. Unlike their predominantly Protestant and British-stock counterparts in the newly independent United States, the citizens of New Orleans were generally Catholic and of French or Spanish stock.

Founded in 1718, New Orleans had flourished as a busy port at the mouth of the Mississippi River, first under the rule of France and then of Spain. By 1788 its population numbered about five thousand. Although no better constructed than the new cities to the east, New Orleans had managed to evade the scourge of a major fire —more through luck than through good planning. That is, until March 21, 1788.

It was Good Friday and the highly Catholic citizenry were observing the occasion with religious solemnity. In the *Vieux Carré,* the heart of the city, candles burned throughout the day in the chapel of a private home. Suddenly one of them fell, setting fire to the lace altarpiece. Soon the draperies were ablaze, setting the whole house on fire. Strong winds picked up the sparks and sent them out across the wooden houses of the quarter. Fortunately no one was killed, but it was an expensive fire.

An eyewitness described the fate of the city:

> ... In order to appreciate the horror of the conflagration, it suffices to say that in less than five hours eight hundred and sixteen buildings were reduced to ashes, comprising in the number all commercial houses except three, and the little that was saved was again lost, or fell prey to malefactors, the unfortunate proprietors barely escaping with their lives. The loss is valued at three millions of dollars. In an affliction so cruel and so general, the only thing that can diminish our grief, is that not a man perished. On the morning of the morrow, what a spectacle was to be seen: in the place of the flourishing city of the day before, nothing but rubbish and heaps of ruins, pale and trembling mothers, dragging their children along by the hand, their despair not

even leaving them the strength to weep or groan; and persons of
luxury, quality, and consideration, who had only a stupor and silence
for their one expression. . . .

New Orleans's luck had clearly run out. Later studies
bemoaned the city's inability to cope with fire:

> . . . when the emergency arose which the experience of other cities
> must have shown them was certain to arise, the best they could do was
> to hunt through the artillery quarters for such military implements as
> were the best adapted to the purpose of staying the progress of the fire
> —a few pioneers' axes, a few military picks, and such implements as
> would enable them to pull down houses and parts of houses that left
> standing might feed the flames with fuel. Apparently not a bucket, and
> certainly no organized preparation to even pass water in buckets to put
> out the fire where it burned, or to wet the roofs that stood in the path
> of the fire.

Lack of equipment was not deemed the only culprit
in the fire. A newspaper of the time also excoriated the
monks of the city for failing to ring the church bells in
alarm, because of an old religious belief:

> . . . the fire taking place on Good Friday, the priests refused to
> allow the alarm to be rung, because on that day all bells must be dumb.
> If such an act of superstition had taken place at Constantinople, it

Plan of the city of New Orleans
showing the area destroyed by the 1794
fire

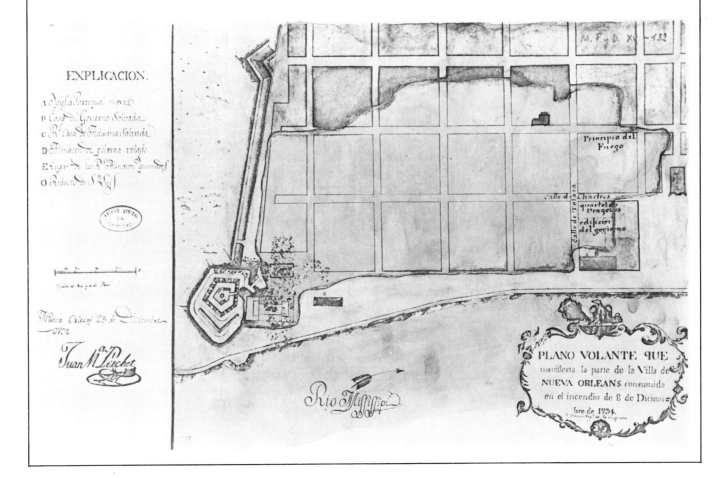

would not have been astonishing. The absurd Mussulman belief in fatality renders sacred to them all the precepts drawn from the Alkoran; but a civilized nation is not made to adopt maxims so culpable towards humanity, and this trait of fanatical insanity will surely not be approved by sensible people.

New Orleans began to rebuild immediately. But this time the chastened city made provision for fire protection. As other communities had done earlier, the townspeople divided the city into four wards. Each one was supplied with buckets and an engine. A commissary of police was appointed to each ward to take charge of the fire equipment, to direct action at fires, and to establish new fire companies as necessary.

RULES FOR VOLUNTEER FIREFIGHTING COMPANIES
NEW YORK, 1802

First, You are to wash and play your engine once every month, as long as the season of the year will permit; and if any fireman is not present when the list is called, he shall pay for every such default one shilling.

Secondly, If any fireman does not appear at his engine before it is brought to the place of playing, he shall pay for every such default two shillings.

Thirdly, If the engine is played out before he appears at the place of playing, or does not appear at all, he shall pay for every such default four shillings.

Fourthly, You are to repair, with the first notice of fire, to your respective engine-house, take your engine and other materials to such fire, there place the same and play the same as you shall be directed by the mayor, recorder, alderman, engineers, or foreman; and be sure that that man who takes pipe or leader does not stir from said engine, under penalty of four shillings for every such default.

Fifthly, After such fire is extinguished, that no fireman absent himself before the said engine and materials belonging thereto are brought to their place; well washed and cleaned before they are put up. Any fireman neglecting his duty in such case shall pay for every such default four shillings.

Sixthly, If any fireman absent himself before he is discharged by one of the engineers, or his foreman, of said engine, shall pay for every such default six shillings.

Seventhly, If any fireman has notice of fire, and hearing by the way of such fire being out, and not coming to his engine-house to see all things put up in order again, shall pay for every such default six shillings.

Eighthly, Any fireman knowing of chimneys being on fire, or is told it by others, and not acquainting his foreman of the name and place within twenty-four hours after he has knowledge of the same, shall pay for every such default ten shillings.

Ninthly, Any foreman being acquainted of such chimneys being on fire by any of his men, or by any

These provisions did not succeed in fully sparing New Orleans from extensive fire damage, for in 1794 fire leveled many of the recently rebuilt structures. But the provisions did serve as a foundation for the establishment of a progressively better organized and efficient firefighting force.

As the 1700s drew to a close, volunteer fire companies were growing more and more important in American community life. It was a badge of honor and a source of great pride to belong to one of these companies, and indeed membership in many of them was limited to the community's leading and most socially prominent citizens.

SECOND GREAT FIRE

NEW ORLEANS
1794

other person, or have it from his own knowledge, and not acquainting the person properly authorized to collect the same within twenty-four hours after his having such knowledge, shall pay for every such default fifteen shillings.

Tenthly, That no excuse be taken for a man's non-attendance to the before-mentioned articles, except confinement by sickness or some other misfortune, or death in a man's family, so as to make it indecent for him to attend.

Lastly, That any fireman neglecting his duty three times successively, unless confinement as before-mentioned should prevent him, shall be struck off the list, and other able-bodied man put in his place.

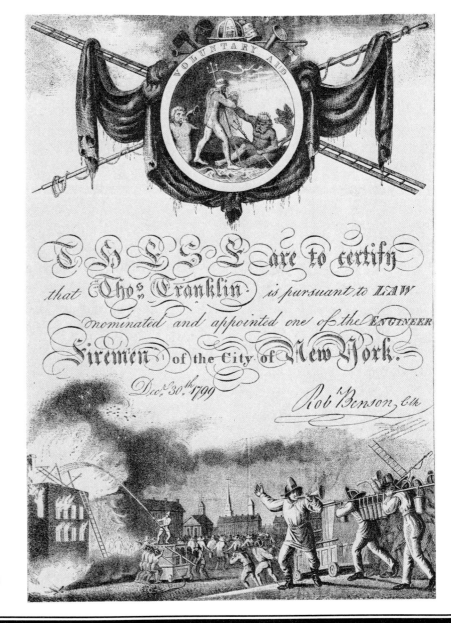

Membership certificate issued to volunteer firefighter Thomas Franklin in New York, 1799

Hibernia Company volunteers in parade dress

THE HIBERNIA FIRE COMPANY

PHILADELPHIA
1790 s

One of the most prestigious and colorful of the volunteer companies was the aforementioned Hibernia Fire Company No. 1, which had supplied so many patriots to fight in the Revolutionary War. Founded in Philadelphia in 1752 and made up largely of men of Irish birth or heritage, it prided itself on having among its members "signers of the Declaration of Independence, ministers, members of Congress, State and national officers, revolutionary chieftains, financiers, merchants, physicians, mechanics, philosophers, and . . . a clergyman."

Rules for members were strict, and breaking them was punishable by fines. For example, the first article of the Hibernians' constitution called for members to "provide two Leathern Buckets, two Baggs and one large Wicker Basket with two handles, the Baggs to be made of Good Oznaburg or wider linen" to be "kept Ready at hand & apply'd to no other use." The second article spelled out the punishment for any who "shall neglect to provide his Buckets, bags & Baskett" or "to keep them ready at hand and in good order in a Convenient place near the street door or shall aply them to any other use." Such an offender "shall forfeit to the use of the Company

& pay unto the Clk. for the time being the sum of two shillings."

The company invariably had its two or three offenders who had to pay up at every meeting: "Mr. Jon McMichal is find for having his baskett with glasses in it in 2 *s.*" (At the next meeting he was fined two shillings "for having Merchandize in his Baskett & but one Bag.") "James Wharton wanted a string in one of his bags" and was similarly fined.

Members were also fined for missing company meetings for too long a time. These meetings were generally held weekly and were deemed necessary so that the men could keep their engine and other equipment in good repair and could keep in practice using it. When this work was done, the men generally got down to serious socializing. Oftentimes the fines were used to help in this last pursuit. Meals and other refreshments were frequently charged against the company's fund.

Fines, as well as assessments on the members, were also used to buy new equipment. In 1790 the Hibernia Company decided that its English-made engine was no longer fit for use, so they contracted with Richard Mason, a maker and seller of fire engines in Philadelphia, to build them a replacement at a cost of £160. Unlike the Newsham engine with its side brakes, the Mason engine was pumped by levers at the front and back and could throw water at a greater distance.

Early Philadelphia-style hand pumper built by Richard Mason could send up a 75-foot stream of water.

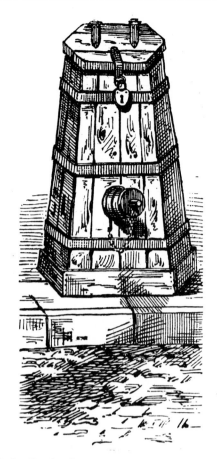

Early fire hydrant

A more powerful engine was just one of many improvements that Philadelphia—along with many other cities—was making in firefighting. By the early 1800s, a system of "trunks," or hollowed-out logs, carried water from the Schuylkill River through the streets of Philadelphia. Fireplugs were fitted into the trunks at strategic spots so that firefighters could get to the water easily.

Wagons to transport hooks and ladders quickly and efficiently were also appearing on the city's streets. Heretofore men had raced to fires carrying their ladders over their shoulders, but now four-wheel carts were being built that could carry not only several ladders, but also hooks, buckets, picks, and fire axes. As such a carriage arrived at the scene of a fire, the cry of "Men up to the roof!" would ring out proudly, and brave hook and ladder firemen would quickly answer the call.

Fire hose was also becoming an important firefighting tool. Although hose had been around for a long time, it was highly ineffective. It was made of sewn leather whose stitches broke easily under pressure. But in 1803 a group of "8 young men" formed the Philadelphia Hose No. 1. After much experimentation, two of its more inventive members, James Sellers and Abraham Pennock, came upon the idea of using rivets instead of stitches.

Hand-drawn hook and ladder wagon, built for the Philadelphia Fire Company in 1799

Above: Nineteenth-century brass nozzle and branch with leather handles.

Top Left: Model of hose wagon built by Patrick Lyon in 1803 for the Philadelphia Hose Company.

Left: Hand-drawn spider-type hose reel built for the Hope Hose Company, Philadelphia, c. 1837

Their new hose was a great success. So was the carriage that fire-engine builder Patrick Lyon designed to carry it. The boxlike six-foot nine-inch by two-foot six-inch structure could transport six hundred feet of hose. Once the hose had been removed, the box itself could be used as a reservoir for water to feed fire engines. Soon another hose carriage appeared, this one a cylinder on two wheels. Called a "jumper" because it could easily be bounced over curbs, it could also carry a great deal more hose. It was soon joined by a four-wheel model with a simple arch frame, called a "spider."

CHARLES DICKENS ON THE AMERICAN VOLUNTEER FIREFIGHTERS

In the mid 1800s the famous English writer Charles Dickens toured the United States, taking notes on what he saw. In 1861 an essay entitled *American Volunteer Firemen* appeared in a literary publication that he edited. The essay makes clear the writer's admiration for the men who worked hard all day and then took on their duties as volunteer firefighters at night. This is how he described them:

"But, after all, it is at night-time that the fireman is really himself, and means something. He lays down the worn-out pen, and shuts up the red-lined ledger. He hurries home . . . slips on his red shirt and black dress-trousers, dons his solid japanned leather helmet bound with brass, and hurries to the guard-room, or the station, if he be on duty.

"A gleam of red, just a blush in the sky, eastward—William-street way—among the warehouses; and presently the telegraph begins to work. For, every fire station has its telegraph, and every street has its line of wires, like metallic washing-lines. Jig-jag, tat-tat, goes the indicator:

" 'Fire in William-street, No. 3, Messrs. Hardcastle and Co.'

"Presently the enormous bell, slung for the purpose in a wooden shed in the City Park just at the end of Broadway, begins to swing and roll backward.

"In dash the volunteers in their red shirts and helmets—from oyster cellars and half-finished clam soup, from newly begun games of bil-liards, from the theatre, from Bouci-cault, from Booth, from the mad drollery of the Christy minstrels, from stiff quadrille parties, from gin-slings, from bar-rooms, from sul-phurous pistol galleries, from stu-dios, from dissecting rooms, from half-shuttered shops, from conver-sazioni and lectures—from every-where—north, south, east, and west —breathless, hot, eager, daring, shouting, mad. Open fly the folding doors, out glides the new engine— the special pride of the company— the engine whose excellence many lives have been lost to maintain; 'A reg'lar high-bred little stepper' as ever smith's hammer forged. It shines like a new set of cutlery, and is as light as a 'spider waggon' or a trotting-gig. It is not the great Jug-gernaut car of our Sun and Phoenix offices—the enormous house on wheels, made as if purposely cum-brous and eternal—but is a mere light musical snuff-box of steel rods and brass supports, with axes and coils of leather, brass-socketed tub-ing fastened beneath, and all ready for instant and alert use.

"Now, the supernumeraries— the haulers and draggers, who lend a hand at the ropes—pour in from the neighboring dram-shops or low dancing-rooms, where they remain waiting to earn some dimes by such casualties. A shout—a tiger!

" 'Hei! hei!! hei!!! hei!!!! (cre-scendo), and out at lightning speed dashes the engine, in the direction of the red gleam now widening . and sending up the fanlike radiance of a volcano.

"Now, a roar and crackle, as the quick-tongued flames leap out, red and eager, or lick the black blistered beams—now, hot belches of smoke from shivering windows—now, snaps and smashes of red-hot beams, as the floors fall in—now, down burning stairs, like frightened mar-tyrs running from the stake, rush poor women and children in white trailing nightgowns—now, the mob, like a great exulting many-headed monster, shouts with delight and sympathy—now, race up the fire-engines, the men defying each other in rivalry, as they plant the ladders and fire-escapes. The fire-trumpets roar out stentorian orders—the red shirts fall into line—rock, rock, go the steel bars that force up the water —up leap the men with the hooks and axes—crash, crash, lop, chop, go the axes at the partitions, where the fire smoulders. Now, spurt up in fluid arches the blue white jets of water, that hiss and splash, and blacken out the spasms of fire; and as every new engine dashes up, the thousands of upturned faces turn to some new shade of reflected crim-son, and the half-broken beams give way at the thunder of their cheers.

"The fire lowers, and is all but subdued, though still every now and then a floor gives way with an earth-quake crash, and into the still lurid dark air rises a storm of sparks like a hurricane of fire-flies. But suddenly there is a crowding together and whispering of helmeted heads. Brave Seth Johnson is missing; all the hook men and axe men are back but he; all the pumpers are there, and all the loafers are there. He alone is missing.

"Caleb Fisher saw him last, shouts the captain to the eager red faces; he was then breaking a third floor back window with his axe. He thinks he is under the last wall that fell. Is there a lad there will not risk his life for Seth? No! or he would be no American, I dare swear.

"Hei! hei!! hei!!! hei!!!!

"Click-shough go the shovels, chick-chick the pickaxes. A shout, a scream of

" 'Seth!'

"He is there, pale and silent, with heaving chest, his breast-bone

Firemen's hall on Fulton Street, New York City, 1824

smashed in, a cold dew oozing from his forehead. Now they bear him to the roaring multitude, their eyes aching and watering with the suffocating gusts of smoke. They lay him pale, in his red shirt, amid the hushed voiceless men in the bruised and scorched helmets. The grave doctor breaks through the crowd. He stoops and feels Seth's pulse. All eyes turn to him. He shakes his head, and makes no other answer. Then the young men take off their helmets and bear home Seth, and some weep, because of his betrothed, and the young men think of her.

"Such are the scenes that occur nightly in New York. The special disgrace of the city is the incessant occurrence of incendiary fires. Yet accidental fires are exceedingly numerous, for wood is still (even in New York) the predominant building material, in consequence of the extraordinary cheapness of wood fit for building. The roofs, too, are generally of tin, and not tile or slate, and this burns through very quickly.

Moreover, the universal stove (derived from the Dutch, I suppose) occasions a great use of flue pipes, and these are buried among wood, and are, even when embedded in stone, dangerous."

It is obvious from the above that much can be learned of the progress and history of Manhattan by following the signal lamps, so to speak, of many generations of the volunteer fire laddies, through the streets of the city. . . . Lead Kindly Light!

Harry Gratacap's fire hat

Cape from Friendship Company, Alexandria, Virginia, said to have been owned by George Washington

The volunteer companies were making strides in guarding the personal safety of their members, too. Hats were pieces of firefighters' garb that needed improvement desperately. One type of early fire hat was the leather jockey cap. Another type was developed by a gunsmith and New York firefighter named Jacob Turck. He devised a leather stovepipe hat with a narrow brim. Many years later, another New York firefighter and hatmaker named Henry T. Gratacap designed the forerunner of the modern fire helmet. It is thought that the idea for it came from the practice of turning round the earlier jockey cap to keep water from running down the firefighter's neck.

Short capes also came into use to protect firefighters' shoulders from falling debris, embers, and water. Made originally of oil cloth, these capes later were made of a piece of canvas covered by three coats of paint, often in the company's colors.

Because of the pride that the volunteers took in their individual companies, they were anxious to show off their membership in them with lavish uniforms, not for firefighting but for parades, picnics, and competitions with other companies. Consequently, firefighting capes evolved from the practical to the purely ornamental.

Another piece of equipment that came into wide use was the fire horn. The company foreman shouted orders to his firefighters through this simple speaking trumpet so that they could hear him above the noise and pandemonium of the fire scene. Through this megaphone he cajoled his men to pump harder and to throw the water farther and faster than the other fire companies on the scene. Just as there were two types of fire uniforms—one for work and one for show—so there were two types of horns. A simple unadorned version was used at a fire, but a more ornate horn was used for awards and presentations. Finely worked, sometimes even jewel-encrusted, it was often awarded to a visiting dignitary or a retiring company member.

During this period, engines were being improved constantly, and Philadelphia (in addition to Boston and Seneca Falls) was one center of fire-engine design and manufacture. The same Philadelphian who had designed the first carriage for his city's Hose No. 1 constructed a new engine for the Hibernia Company. Although built on the same principle as the earlier Mason engine, Pat Lyon's machine was larger and more powerful. While only two men were required to pump the Mason engine, one on either handle, the Lyon engine used four rows of men pumping, two rows of them at each of the double-handled brakes, one on the ground and one on a platform across the width of the engine. This design, with the pumping brakes at the front and back of the engine, came to be called the "Philadelphia style," and soon "Philadelphia engines" were being used in cities up and down the eastern seaboard.

The largest producer of hand engines during this time was the Wm. C. Hunneman Company of Boston. A coppersmith by trade, Hunneman built 716 pumpers that were used as far from Boston as South America.

Unfortunately the developing communities farther inland were not as well equipped as the east coast for firefighting. Fire was just as formidable an opponent to them as it had been to the Colonial settlements. Detroit became one case in point. A frontier port and trading post since 1701, it was finally turned over by the British to the United States in 1796, when it had twenty-five hundred inhabitants. By 1805 the population was still growing, but fire nearly put an end to Detroit. On June 11 a stable caught on fire, and the flames raged through the town as they had through so many American towns before. All day long the people of Detroit fought the blaze, along with volunteer firefighters who had sailed across Lake St. Clair from Windsor, Canada. But by day's end the entire town, with the exception of two buildings, was destroyed.

Thanks to the help of the United States government and nearby communities, Detroit recovered and rebuilt. By 1812 it was flourishing enough to make it once more attractive to the British. In that year, near the start of the War of 1812, the British regained control of Detroit.

As in the Revolutionary War, fire was used as a weapon in this war. Probably the most notable example was the British firing of Washington, D.C., in 1814. Knowing that the British troops were sailing up the Chesapeake Bay toward them, ninety-nine percent of the federal city's residents left the city. The handful of American troops standing guard knew that they were no match for the British force, so they too retreated.

Soon after the invaders landed, their commander ordered that they put the public buildings to the torch. Redcoats soon fired the Capitol, the White House (from which Dolly Madison, wife of President James Madison, had fled only a few hours before, clutching some state

Fire horns: presentation (left) and working (right) from the 19th century

STABLE FIRE

DETROIT
1805

BRITISH BURNING OF CAPITOL

WASHINGTON, D.C.
1814

Philadelphia-style engine, 1811

Engine jack used to prop up machine when, as frequently happened, a wheel broke

STABLE FIRE

SAVANNAH
1820

papers and a painting of George Washington hastily hacked from its frame), the Treasury Department, the War Department, and a Government arsenal. (This last firing was more costly to the British than to the Americans since an explosion of hidden ammunition killed at least a hundred of their soldiers.)

The British act was severely criticized both in the United States and in Great Britain as a vindictive and unnecessary one, since Washington was not defended and since taking it was not a decisive step in the war. The London *Times,* though, did not agree. It stated that the action was completely justified, as it had achieved two objectives—"the destruction of a most formidable naval arsenal belonging to the enemy, and a retribution which should have the effect of stopping the barbarities authorized and encouraged by the American Government."

Because of its superior naval force (something like 475 ships), Great Britain was able to extend a naval blockade all the way down the eastern seaboard during the War of 1812. One of the American ports victimized by the blockade was Savannah, Georgia. The city was spared invasion and therefore escaped Washington's fate of a costly fire. But in 1820 a major fire did envelop the city. As in Detroit fifteen years earlier, a stable was the scene of its start. Nearly half of the eighty-year-old city was destroyed—about five hundred dwellings. Fortunately, many of its eighteenth- and early nineteenth-century stately homes escaped destruction, and are preserved today as part of Historic Savannah.

As the nation continued its vast westward growth during the 1800s, everything about firefighting was growing as well—the number of fire companies, the size and power of fire engines, firefighters' pride and rivalry over their "masheens," and the size and financial losses of city fires.

Across the continent volunteer fire companies were springing up wherever frontier settlements were developing into towns and cities. They gave themselves colorful names such as the Golden Gulch Company, of Carson City, Nevada, and nicknames and mottoes: the Confidence Company of Sacramento, California, called themselves the "Roosters" and proclaimed "Douse the Glim." Their neighbor the Protection Company called themselves the "Honey Bees" and had as their cry "Duty tho' in Peril." All of these companies were organized along the same lines as their counterparts in the East and South.

Many of the new companies chose Philadelphia-style engines. Others decided on the increasingly popular "New York style," which was built on the old Newsham principle of pumping brakes at the sides rather than at the front and back of the engine. It required as many men to pump water as the Philadelphia style engine, or sometimes even more.

Volunteer firefighters at work in mid 19th century

New York-style engine, with pumping brakes at sides

The New York style probably reached its most powerful with the development of the so-called Mankiller. It was a very heavy engine with double-deck side brakes that, when folded, stood high above the machine and gave her the added nickname of "Haywagon." But it was her operation rather than her appearance that earned her the name "Mankiller." Difficult to pump, she quickly exhausted one set of men and demanded another set in their place.

The care the men took of their masheen, or the "Old Gal" as she was often called, was nothing short of loving and lavish. Her brass fittings had to be polished to a high sheen. Her wood had to be rubbed to a high gloss. And of course all working parts had to be perfectly oiled and in tune.

An engine also had to reflect the taste and identity of its company. The men would appoint a painting committee that would in turn commission a painter to work out a color scheme for their pumper and to adorn her with pointed panels of classical or patriotic scenes. Such decoration sometimes earned the machines their affectionate nicknames—"Old Wreath of Roses" and "Black Joke," for example.

The fierce pride the volunteer firefighters took in the appearance of their machinery was more than matched by their pride in its use. It was a point of honor to be the first company to reach and "get first water" at a fire, and often there was a money prize given by an insurance company (if the property was insured) for being first. But for whatever reason, every company would do all it could to reach a fire before its rivals, and "all it could" often covered a multitude of sins.

Sometimes as soon as a company heard an alarm, they would send a small boy running ahead to the scene of the fire while they got in harness to pull their engine through the streets. The fleet-footed boy's job was to cover the water supply nearest the fire with a barrel, or in some other way obscure it, so that his company could get first water even though they were not first on the scene. Or one company racing down the street and finding itself behind another company might jump their

Membership certificates from fire companies in Philadelphia (below) and Danvers, Massachusetts (overleaf)

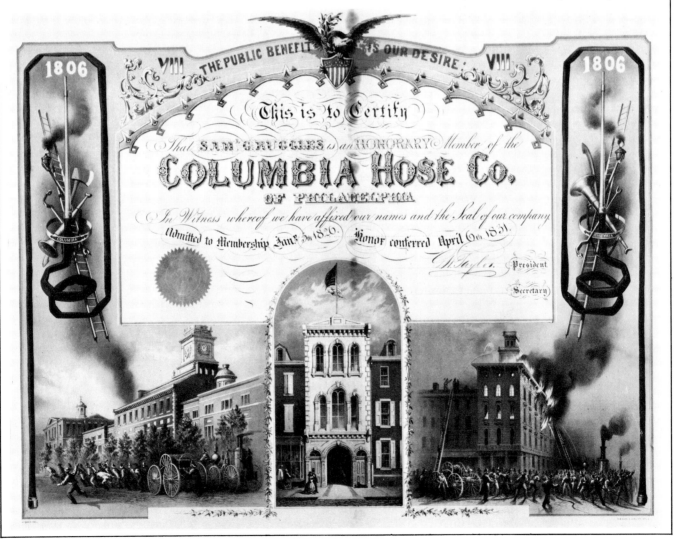

Danvers Fire Department.

THIS CERTIFIES,

That _____ is a Member of Engine Company No. _ and is entitled to all the privileges and exemptions of Enginemen, for and during one year, unless this Certificate shall be sooner revoked.

_____ Secretary. _____ President.

DANVERS, _____ 183_

engine up on the sidewalk, at the peril of pedestrians, and pass their rival. "Passing" another engine on the way to a fire was a triumph for any company just as "being passed" was disgrace. Fist fights were not uncommon between companies vying for the honor of "first in."

Having finally arrived at a fire, the men were anxious to show the superiority of their engine and their use of it. Often the fire was a good distance from the water supply, whether it was a river, spring, cistern, or hydrant. In such cases the engines would form a line. The first company on the scene would put one of its hoses into the supply and start pumping water into its machine. When the next company arrived, the first would ask "Will you take our water?" It would then extend its other hose, perhaps 150 to 200 feet long, to the second engine and start filling it. The men on that engine would in turn pump the water their engine was receiving through a hose to the next engine, and so on until the water could be played on the fire.

This system also provided an opportunity for triumph or disgrace. To keep the water flowing constantly from engine to engine required that each company pump at about the same rate and move the same amount of water. If one engine slowed down, it was in immediate danger of being "washed"—that is, the engine behind it could overflow it and thus show superiority of strength, stamina, and masheen.

Fire companies took very great care to keep track of who was washed and who avoided this disgrace. A new engine was considered "a virgin" until another company succeeded in washing it. For obvious reasons then, one volunteer company took extravagant pride in the name that the spotless reputation of their masheen earned herself—"Old Maid."

Rivalry among companies was not limited to their work at actual fire scenes. Companies often set up competitions at fairs or picnics or musters to prove which of them could pump faster, throw water farther, scale a wall more quickly, and so on. A favorite competition involved proving who could throw water higher. A church steeple or the cupola of a public building—possibly 125 feet high—was frequently used as the measuring stick, and each company, madly pumping—perhaps at a killing pace of 140 strokes a minute, or over twice the normal rate—would shoot its stream skyward and compare the heights reached.

One such competition took place around a liberty pole that had been constructed outside Tom Riley's Fifth Ward Hotel in New York City. One of the competitors was Americus Engine Company No. 6, whose foreman was the famous William Marcy Tweed, who has become the working symbol for corrupt politics. Americus proved themselves the best, reaching to within three feet of the top of the pole. Full of his company's victory and mindful of good wagering possibilities, Tweed stated that the next day his men would not only reach the top of the pole but would also send water over it. To insure victory Tweed hired a sailor to climb the pole that night under cover of darkness, and cut six feet off the top of the pole. For this climbing feat, the sailor was to receive ten dollars—five down and five when the job was done. The next day the confident Americus Company manned "Big 6," the bright red Philadelphia-style engine that John Agnew had built for them, and started to pump mightily. But for all their work the stream did not rise over the top of the pole. Angrily Tweed confronted the sailor only to be calmly informed that since only half of the fee had been paid, only half of the job—the removal of three feet, not six—had been done.

The insignia of the Americus Fire Company in New York City carried on the engine "Big Six"

THE GREAT NEW YORK FIRE OF 1835

NEW YORK
1835

Firefighting may have offered such social diversions, but it continued to present danger and physical strain as well. New York fire companies had more of both than it seemed possible to stand in 1835, culminating with a mammoth battle against their enemy at year's end.

"December 17, 1835—How shall I record the events of last night, or how attempt to describe the most awful calamity which has ever visited the United States?" With these words the prominent New Yorker Philip Hone struggled to begin an eyewitness account of his city's Great Fire of 1835, the most destructive nonmilitary fire the world had known since London was turned to ashes in 1666.

"I am fatigued in body, disturbed in mind, and my fancy filled with images of horror which my pen is inadequate to describe," he continued. "Nearly one-half of the first ward is in ashes, five hundred to seven hundred stores, which, with their contents, are valued at $20,000,000 to $40,000,000, are now lying in an indistinguishable mass of ruins. There is not, perhaps, in the world the same space of ground covered by so great an amount of

MOLLY,
ENGINE COMPANY NO. 11
NEW YORK, NEW YORK

LILLIE HITCHCOCK COIT,
KNICKERBOCKER ENGINE COMPANY NO. 5
SAN FRANCISCO, CALIFORNIA

and MARINA BETTS
PITTSBURGH, PENNSYLVANIA

Lillie Coit

While "running with the volunteers" is remembered as strictly a male avocation, there were a few highly colorful female exceptions.

One was Molly, a slave who belonged to a member of New York's Engine Company No. 11. At the sound of the alarm, Molly would answer right along with him. She took her work seriously and was proud to be "as good a fire laddie as many of the boys who bragged at being such." She is best remembered for the night a fire broke out during a blizzard in 1818. Only a few volunteers were able to get through to answer the alarm, so Molly took hold of the drag-rope with them and began to pull on it "for dear life," struggling to draw the pumper through the virtually impassable snow. From that point on, Molly would say of herself,

real and personal property as the scene of this dreadful conflagration."

The fire that so distressed Hone had been spotted at nine o'clock in the evening of December 16. A fire insurance watchman saw smoke coming from a five-story dry-goods building in a highly commercial area south of Wall Street. As soon as he turned in the alarm, the bells in City Hall and in nearby churches began clanging, their peals calling to the fire companies and telling where the fire was located.

The company nearest to the fire, Engine No. 11, tried to respond to the call, but they could not. In the 17°-below-zero weather, their engine had frozen. In an attempt to thaw it they lighted a fire below it. But the attempt was too successful, for not only did the engine

42

"I belongs to ole 'Leven; I allers runs wid dat old bull-gine."

Another female "laddie" was Marina Betts, a resident of Pittsburgh's Shinbone Alley in the 1820s. A formidable woman of five feet ten inches, she was described in such terms as "virago" and "recruiting sergeant." As soon as a fire was discovered, Marina would be there, joining the bucket brigade and seeing that everyone nearby joined it too. "Woe to the dandy who passed or stood as a spectator when, as Marina said, 'Menfolks should be working.' He would get the contents of the next full bucket she caught. . . . She was more effective in securing workers than half a dozen captains, for those out of reach of her bucket would feel the weight of her tongue if she perceived any signs of skulking, and few dared to brave the ordeal of either." So Marina Betts was remembered fifty years later in Pittsburgh.

During the mid-1800s a third firefighting female took up the drag-ropes in San Francisco, this one a socialite and one of the wealthiest heiresses in the Bay City. Fifteen-year-old Lillie Hitchcock was on her way home from school one day when she saw a short-handed company of volunteers trying to run their engine up Telegraph Hill to a fire. Of course they were falling behind the other companies, so the impulsive Lillie grabbed a vacant place at the ropes and shouted, "Come on, you men! Let's beat 'em." According to one account: "The Knickerbocker No. 5 shot up the slope like a streak, beat the other volunteers, and got first water on the fire."

Lillie said of herself that she "loved courage in a uniform," and the men of Knickerbocker No. 5 loved her courage too; they made her an honorary member. From then on she was expected to attend every fire, where "No. 5 always regarded her presence worth more than that of many men, for they redoubled their efforts when she stood looking on with pride at the work of 'her company.'"

Upon her marriage she gave up her fire work, but until her death she wore a little gold 5 pinned to her dress (solid gold, of course), and she signed herself "Lillie H. Coit 5."

thaw—it also caught on fire, and within a short while the engine, as well as the firehouse, lay in ruins. The disconsolate No. 11 volunteers turned from the embers and raced to join other, still equipped, companies in fighting the fire.

Actually, the first of these companies had arrived at the scene within ten minutes of the alarm—against great odds. The men had fought two "heavy fires" only two nights before and several small ones the preceding night; many of them were "almost fagged out." Then too, deep snow and the bitter cold made pulling the engines a nearly impossible task.

Once the companies began to arrive, they found the fire hydrants frozen, leading them to try for water from the nearby East River. But the river was also frozen, so the determined men moved their engines out onto it and chopped holes through the ice, into which they dropped their hoses. Then the companies strung the engines out, forming a line three blocks long. The men pumped incessantly, knowing that the slightest pause could allow their engine as well as their hose to freeze up. But even when the water was finally forced within streaming distance of the fire, it was largely useless. Gale winds threw it back in the firefighters' faces, forming icicles on their helmets and a sheet of ice on their coats.

Seeing the terrible extent of the emergency, "Handsome Jim" Gulick, Chief Engineer, called out the rest of his department. Soon all forty-nine engines, five hose carts, and six hook and ladder trucks were joined in the battle—against the flames, against the ice, and against the molten metal that poured down on the firefighters as iron shutters and copper roofs melted in the blaze.

Firefighters battle flames in New York's Great Fire of 1835

FIRE AS ENTERTAINMENT

Large-scale fires periodically ravaged great portions of eighteenth- and nineteenth-century New York, and New Yorkers became inured to the holocausts that often gutted the city. Moreover, "fires were so frequent in New York that visitors regarded them as one of the city's tourist sights." Commenting on this predicament, a visitor from Sweden noted in the 1840s:

When the fire breaks out tonight . . . we'll go out and take a look at it. It was like deciding to go to the theater to see a play that had been announced and that could be counted on with certainty to come off. And sure enough, we did not have long to wait for the spectacle.

New Yorkers enjoy the spectacle.

Merchants madly tried to save their goods, moving them to locations they thought safe, only to watch those places go up in flames too. Cases of champagne and barrels of liquor were carried off, unceremoniously broken open, and guzzled by the throngs around the fire. Ironically, they also hauled expensive furniture out of buildings and broke it up as fuel for fires to keep themselves warm.

The flames could be seen a hundred miles away, and companies from surrounding communities—Brooklyn and White Plains in New York and Morristown, Newark, and Hoboken in New Jersey—rushed to New York's aid. Even Philadelphia was not too far away to send help, and four hundred Philadelphia firefighters loaded their equipment on a train and headed for the stricken city.

By this time Chief Gulick knew that the only way to stop the fire's progress was to create firebreaks. Navy officers and men, and a gang of miners, were directed to locate the necessary explosives. With great courage and cool-headedness they raced through showers of fire, kegs of gunpowder wrapped in their coats, and set their charges in the buildings Gulick indicated.

Finally, by noon of December 17, fifteen hours after the fire had begun, a firebreak was made. Fires continued to smolder throughout the seventeen-block area, but the worst was over. Amazingly only one death resulted from the fire—the crowd had found a man setting a fire, whether out of lunacy or drunkenness no one inquired, and promptly lynched him. The economic consequences of the fire were thoroughly devastating. The losses suffered, and the unwise loans made to try to restore them, led to the Wall Street Panic of 1837, which resulted in the most serious depression America had suffered up to that time.

SPERM-OIL FIRE

NEW YORK
1845

Ten years later a great fire again struck New York, but this time it did cause heavy loss of life—thirty people perished, four of them firefighters. Explosives were the cause of much of the death and destruction at this fire. Flames that had begun at three o'clock in the morning of July 20, 1845, in a sperm oil establishment near the scene of the fire of 1835, moved down to a building in which saltpeter, a substance used in making gunpowder, was stored. Within ten minutes "it blew up, the shock breaking a million panes of glass throughout the whole city." The explosion left "not a vestige of the edifice . . . except the bricks" and it demolished six or seven adjoining buildings. It blew the heavy doors off several banks in the area. It slivered fire engines nearby to atoms, killing at least one firefighter and literally sending another one along with the part of the roof he was sitting on, flying across the street. Incredibly, he lived to tell about it. This is how firefighter Francis Hart, Jr., described his impossible-sounding experience.

I was at the fire on the 19th instant; and was with the pipe of No. 22 on the rear of the fourth story of the chair factory in Broad Street, when that building took fire. An alarm being given, preparations were made to take down the pipe. I remained to light down the hose, and when I undertook to go down the flame and smoke were so great as to prevent my descending, and I went on the roof of the chair factory. I went along from that building to the corner of Broad and Exchange Streets, breaking each skylight as I proceeded over the roofs, but found no stairs leading from such skylights. Finding myself thus on the third building from the chair factory, without any means of getting down, I sat in the scuttle. I did not then consider myself in any danger. I had been there about five minutes when I heard the first explosion—a species of rumbling sound—followed by a succession of others of the same kind. The gable of the house next to the corner shook with the first and each successive explosion, so that I had prepared myself, if it threatened to fall, to jump through the scuttle of the corner house. After the small explosions the great explosion took place, the noise of which seemed to be principally below me. I perceived the flames shooting across the street. I felt the building falling under me, and the roof moved around so that a corner of it caught in the opposite side of Exchange Street, and was thrown off into Exchange Street, but without any serious injury to my person. As far as I could judge, the whole roof that I was on moved in one piece, and the walls under it crumbled down beneath it. I think there were some fifteen or eighteen small explosions. I could see our engine from the roof I was on, and know that the explosions occurred in 38 Broad Street. None of the explosions, before the great one, came through, or disturbed any of the roofs of houses in Broad Street.

The 1845 fire destroyed part of the commercial area rebuilt after the 1835 fire, as well as many homes of the poor. In all, damage was estimated at three hundred buildings and $6 to $10 million (between about $37.5 and $62.5 million today).

Only two months before fire ravaged New York, it had destroyed one third of a rapidly growing city to the west. Pittsburgh's development had paralleled that of her eastern sisters. Wooden buildings, often cheaply and haphazardly constructed, had been crowded together near a river. Such construction had often invited devastating fires in other cities, and on April 10, 1845, a windy day following two weeks without rain, the invitation in Pittsburgh was accepted.

At noon on that day a woman named Mrs. Zeigler stood outdoors at her washtub, heating the water for her laundry. The wind picked up sparks and sent them into a nearby frame building. Within minutes the windswept flames were racing from building to building. The city's volunteer fire companies arrived at the scene quickly, but the low water supply made it impossible to control the

THE GREAT FIRE

PITTSBURGH
1845

Pittsburgh after the great 1845 fire

flames. Attempts to blow up buildings to make a firebreak also came to naught because the fire was spreading so rapidly that it was impossible to lay a trail of gunpowder from a building before it went up in flames.

Finally, after five hours, the fire simply ran out of fuel and burned itself out. Fifty-six acres of homes, offices, and warehouses—a thousand buildings in all—were in ruins. Estimates of the loss ran from $6 million to $12 million ($37.5 to $75 million today). A few years later, a writer described the scene:

> After dark might have been seen, in every direction, families without shelter guarding such portions of their furniture as they were able to save from the flames, and not knowing where to lay their heads, or get a morsel of food. Frightful as was the progress of the flames, and terrible as the havoc seemed while the fire was raging, no one could realize the losses and privations the citizens sustained until they had walked through the forest of chimneys which marked the path of the destroying element. Merchants, mechanics, workingmen, all, all were ruined. That night ruin struck hundreds of families in the face who had arisen in the morning with plenty of this world's goods, and they found no place whereon to lay their heads, or even food for their children. Men, who the day before were worth their thousands to-day were bankrupt.

The same words might have been used to describe the scene in St. Louis four years later. In 1849 the "Gateway to the West" was a busy place indeed. The narrow streets were alive with Forty-niners being outfitted for

PIER AND WAREHOUSE FIRE

ST. LOUIS
1849

their trek to the gold fields of California. Steamers bringing goods from up and down the Mississippi lined the levee. Late in the evening of May 17 one of them, the *White Cloud,* caught (or possibly was set) on fire. The flames leapt across to the levee, setting the wooden planks and the goods on them afire. Soon the boats surrounding the *White Cloud,* unable to get up enough steam to escape, were also ablaze. One steamer broke away from its mooring and began to drift downstream, colliding with still more steamers and setting them afire as it did. Within half an hour the levee was in flames for a solid mile.

The fire raced westward from the river, taking with it many well-stocked warehouses. Block after block—fifteen in all—became a mass of flame. The business district was completely burnt out. In an attempt to stop the spread, firefighters blew up six buildings. Finally the fire burned itself out. When dawn broke, three square miles of the city were in ashes and twenty-three steamers, along with countless other riverboats, lay smoldering on the Mississippi. More than four hundred buildings and $6 million (about $37.5 million today) had been lost.

By the time the people of St. Louis began to rebuild their city, they had learned several lessons. They made their new streets wider and their structures more resistant to fire.

Steamboats blaze as crowds watch during St. Louis fire in 1849.

CAPTAIN THOMAS B. TARGEE

MISSOURI FIRE COMPANY
ST. LOUIS, MISSOURI

Perhaps no job in firefighting was more dangerous at the time of the St. Louis fire than setting explosives in buildings to establish firebreaks. A keg of gunpowder was used as the explosive, and running such a volatile agent through the flames, setting a trail of gunpowder from it, lighting it, and getting out in time was extremely perilous.

That was the job Thomas Targee, captain and president of the Missouri Fire Company, took on not once but three times during the course of the St. Louis fire. Having set the explosives in two buildings, Targee headed for a third. An eyewitness, a friend of Targee's, gave this account of what followed:

I was watching the flames, mounted on my horse, in front of the Market House. It was a grand and terrible sight, and it seemed that all the gallant efforts of the firemen must prove ineffectual to save the city from complete destruction.

While I watched, I saw Captain Targee, smoke-begrimed and haggard through his grime, stagger and run past me with a keg of gunpowder on his shoulder.

"Where are you going, Captain?" I asked him.

Scarcely pausing, he answered: "We are going to blow up Phillip's Store."

And he passed on. That was the last I ever saw of poor Targee. While I watched I saw men in the smoke-filled street rush ahead of Targee and with kicks and blows from their axes batter in the door of the music store. Then Targee entered. Almost immediately there was a terrific report. Before I could turn my horse's head to retreat I saw an object descending and with a sickening impact it fell at my horse's feet.

I looked down and saw the bleeding leg of the gallant fire captain, which had been severed just at the thigh.

Targee had been blown to bits. What went wrong was never determined. Perhaps explosives had already been set in the building and they went off as he entered. Or perhaps the bung was missing from the keg under his arm, and flames reached the powder. Whatever the cause St. Louis had suffered its first loss of a firefighter killed in the line of duty. The men of the Missouri Company reverently gathered up the shattered body of their captain and buried him simply. He had done his job: the building in which he was killed was the vanishing point of the fire. There it finally stopped its long march of devastation.

Starting with the St. Louis destruction, fire seemed to dog the footsteps of the Forty-niners. Late in 1849 a series of fires began to plague the city for which many of them were headed—San Francisco.

The discovery of gold in the Sacramento Valley in 1848 had caused San Francisco to burgeon from a town of two thousand to a thriving city of forty thousand in only six months. This new population was made up almost exclusively of gold seekers, but not all of them wanted to prospect for gold by digging or panning. A sizable number of them—gamblers, shysters, and schemers—were more interested in prospecting the prospectors.

A gang of these low lifes banded together in a powerful organization called the "Hounds." Their own peculiar methods of panning for gold included cheating, stealing, murder—and arson. The fires they set in commercial areas gave them a truly "golden" opportunity to loot stores and warehouses of their goods. Between December 24, 1849, and June 22, 1851, this "lawless gang of desperadoes" visited six major fires on San Francisco, each one more terrible and extensive than the last until the final one destroyed nearly the entire city.

By 1851 San Franciscans, who had rebuilt as quickly as they were burnt out, had clearly had enough. They formed a Committee of Vigilance and set out to destroy the "Hounds." Using the rough frontier justice of western vigilantes, they rounded up and "tried" gang members. Punishment was generally a swift hanging. It was not long before the Committee of Vigilance had rid San Francisco of its arsonists—along with a few innocents caught up in the reforming fervor. The city was now free to build and expand and flourish for the next fifty years—until an earthquake would destroy it.

To the north of San Francisco, the city of Sacramento was also feeling the influx of Forty-niners. Like San Francisco, Sacramento was composed of wood and canvas buildings that made it a tinder box. In 1850 concerned citizens began to agitate for the organization of a fire protection system. The City Council concurred and within a year Sacramento had provided for four engine companies and one hook and ladder company, made up of civic-minded young volunteers and equipped with apparatus funded by the City Council and by public subscription. A series of cisterns was also constructed to make water more readily available to the firefighters.

ARSON GANG

SAN FRANCISCO
1849–1851

WIND + DROUGHT = FIRE DEVASTATION

SACRAMENTO
1852

But the night of November 2, 1852, proved that the system was not sufficient to the city's needs. A fire broke out in a millinery shop, and two invincible enemies of firefighting—a gale wind and a scarcity of water—made it impossible to stop. As the *City Directory* reported it:

> So rapid was the spread of the fire, and so intense its heat, that step by step they [the firefighters] were forced to retreat before it, until they were driven entirely beyond its reach.
>
> The wind now heightened to a gale, and catching the sparks as they were borne high in the air, carried them into distant portions of the city and dropped them among inflammable material where, in turn, they communicated their destructive power to other buildings, and added to the terror of the awful panorama, by presenting detached walls of flame in a dozen different localities.

By dawn, seven thousand buildings, nearly the whole city, were in ashes and thirteen thousand people were homeless. According to one eyewitness:

> In the brief space of seven hours, the city was seemingly blotted out of existence. The next morning so far as the eye could reach, one black charred mass of ruins greeted it. Men, women and children roamed amidst its desolation, houseless, homeless and destitute. Hardly a place was left by the destroyer to supply them with the necessaries of life.

The fire companies were dismayed at their lack of success. A writer described Sacramento Engine Company No. 3, three of whose men had been buried in a roof cave-in and had been burned to death, the morning of November 3:

> A few members of the Company tired, sick at heart, and almost despairing, dragged their Engine slowly down I Street and left her in front of what was once their House but now a heap of ruins. For three months she laid there, exposed to the elements and partially buried in the mud.

But the citizens of Sacramento pulled themselves together and went to work. Entire buildings were disassembled in San Francisco and several upriver towns and shipped to the stricken city, where they were quickly reassembled. In only one month Sacramento was "again built up, presenting its former proportions of boundary, and numbering nearly as many buildings as occupied it previous to the fiery visitation. Trade nothing diminished pours its tributes through all the usual avenues, and gives promise of a more flourishing condition of things than ever." So said the *Sacramento Steamer Union*.

The original fire companies were reorganized and new ones were established. Within a short time the volunteer companies were restored to their old selves—so that they could once again take up the beginning traditions of firefighting, socializing, and rivalry.

On the East Coast, New York City was also suffering a series of severe fires during the 1850s. Three fires in particular took their toll—the first of the lives of eleven firefighters, the second of a priceless art collection, and the third of the lives of twenty tenement dwellers.

The first of these tragic fires began on April 25, 1854, at eight o'clock in the evening in the W. T. Jennings and Company clothing store. Several firefighters rushed into the store in an attempt to put out the flames. They did not know that above them was a heavy safe. It soon came crashing down through the floor, instantly killing two of them. With that, an iron arch that supported the rear wall cracked and sent the wall crashing over the rest of the men, burying about twenty-five of them. Among them was a young firefighter named Daniel McKay. His brother Alexander and many other firefighters on the scene

THE JENNINGS FIRE

NEW YORK
1854

Fire at the W. T. Jennings and Company clothing store, New York City, 1854. Eleven firemen died here.

rushed to dig out their comrades, but the flames and the scalding water from the hose nozzles turned on the building made their task almost impossible.

By one o'clock in the morning the fire was over and four men had been removed dead from the cellar. Shortly thereafter the firefighters heard a voice from the cellar, that of their twenty-one-year-old comrade John O'Donnell, the son of the City Coroner. He reported that there were six men lying dead near him. The exhausted firefighters finally succeeded in rescuing him, but it was too late. He died in New York Hospital that night.

Also among the eleven dead were both the McKay brothers and Andy Schenck, who had a few hours earlier been spending the evening with the young woman he was about to marry. When the alarm went out she begged him not to respond to it. "No," he replied, "I'll go to this fire, and this is the last fire I will go to." And indeed it was.

Subsequent investigations found not only that the building had been of poor construction, but that it also had been set afire by thieves, three of whom were found and sent to State Prison.

In the year before the Jennings fire, New York had been the scene of the Great World's Fair of 1853. For the event, a spectacular steel-framework and glass-domed building—the Crystal Palace—had been constructed to house the exhibitions. A writer of the period described it as follows:

> The fairy-like Greek cross of glass, bound together with withes of iron, with its graceful galleries, filled with choice productions of art and manufactures, gathered from the most distant parts of the earth, quaint old armor from the Tower of London, gossamer fabrics from the looms of Cashmere, Sèvres china, Gobelin tapestry, Indian curiosities, stuffs, jewelry, musical instruments, carriages, and machinery of home and foreign manufacture, Marochetti's colossal statue of Washington, Kiss's Amazon, Thorwaldsen's Christ and the Apostles, Powers's Greek Slave, and a host of other works of art beside, will long be remembered as the most tasteful ornament that ever graced the metropolis.

THE CRYSTAL PALACE FIRE

NEW YORK
1858

But on October 5, 1858, fire made short work of this monument to art and industry. At about five o'clock in the evening as two thousand people strolled its galleries, smoke was discovered near an entrance. At the cry of "Fire," all two thousand rushed to the exits, some as far as a block away. The flames raced across the wooden floors, the broad aisles acting as flues driving them on.

The dome of New York's Crystal Palace collapses during its destruction by fire in 1858.

Firefighters were on the scene almost immediately, training twenty or thirty streams of water on the flames. But their efforts accomplished little. Within twelve minutes, 39,000 square feet of glass and 1,250 tons of iron came crashing down on countless art treasures and other exhibitions. Mercifully no lives were lost, although it might have been a different story if the fire had started a few hours later—ten thousand people would have been attending a concert in the Crystal Palace. Once again arsonists were blamed for the fire, but this time they were not caught.

Loss of life was not avoided in the Elm Street tenement fire on February 2, 1860, however. The tenement—a building of six or seven stories containing many living units—had been designed as a profitable way of housing many people on one relatively small piece of land. Living conditions in the units were often crowded, dark, and unsanitary, but the poor, having nowhere else to go, huddled there and made the best of life as it came.

That was the role of the tenement at No. 142 Elm Street in downtown New York City. And on that February day its tenants found out something else about the living conditions there—they were very dangerous. That day twenty of them either jumped or were burned to

THE ELM STREET TENEMENT FIRE

NEW YORK
1860

Ladders fail to reach trapped victims during the Elm Street tenement fire in New York City, 1860.

death as the tenement went up in flames, for the buildings had been built much higher than the reach of the Fire Department's ladders. There would have been many more victims if several firefighters had not valiantly saved a number of them.

The tragedy on Elm Street did have one good effect. It moved the City Council to order that all such buildings have fire escapes that could be reached from all rooms. The order came too late for the residents of No. 142, but it no doubt has saved countless other lives.

During this same period, the 1850s, many innovations were being made in firefighting equipment. The Industrial Revolution now began to affect firefighting. The conversion from man-drawn, man-pumped "enjines" to steam-powered, horse-drawn "bulljines" was underway—much to the angry dismay of the dedicated volunteers and to the heartfelt relief of insurance companies and many concerned citizens.

Rivalries between volunteer companies had reached their highest pitch at midcentury. In cities across the country, fire companies had swollen to fifty or eighty men apiece, and too many of them seemed more interested in fighting each other than in firefighting. Drinking and violence at fires were all too common. So was looting by people attached to the fire companies. At times the behavior of the volunteer companies at fires was so objectionable that they were ordered by city authorities "to turn tongue in"—to suspend all firefighting work.

Cincinnati was one of the first cities in which the situation came to a head. In 1851 two companies en route to a fire at a planing mill met at an intersection and a fist fight broke out. Before long, ten companies were involved in the brawl. Meanwhile the neglected fire raged on and totally destroyed the mill. Angry insurance companies, who, after all, bore the brunt of such losses, demanded action. So did angry citizens who had been harassed and sometimes cheated by the "plug uglies" among the volunteers.

Actually insurance companies had been trying for years to have the hand pumpers, whose operation required large companies of men, replaced by steam pumpers, which required only three men to operate. A successful steam fire engine had been developed in England in 1829, and insurance companies in New York commis-

FIREFIGHTERS' BRAWL
CINCINNATI
1851

Left: Competition among firefighters was not confined to racing to fires. Here "Fire Laddies" stretch hose at a tournament in the mid 19th century.

Above: The foreman urges his men on with his fire horn.

Equipment and spectators gather at a fire in Cincinnati in the mid 19th century.

sioned an American engineer, Paul R. Hodge, to build a workable model for the United States. He succeeded in 1840 and 1841, but the machine so antagonized the volunteers—with its threat to their beloved companies—that the insurance people backed away and sold it to a box factory. After all, the insurance companies had to rely on the volunteer firemen. Even firefighting that was sometimes poor, after all, was better than no firefighting at all.

But Cincinnati did not give up so easily. After the planing mill incident, the City Council appropriated five thousand dollars for the development of a steam fire engine. They commissioned Moses Latta to do the job. He and his two brothers succeeded at their task, and on March 2, 1852, they presented their engine for public tests.

As a crowd watched, one man, the stoker, struck a handful of matches and thrust them into the kindling under the boiler. Then he threw some cannel coal—a quick-burning, hot fuel—into the lighted kindling. As the boiler started heating, the stoker and the engine driver attached a suction hose to the water supply and a few hose-wagon men coupled their hose to the engine. The steamer was ready for action. At the cry of "Water," the engineer opened the throttle, and the machine went to work. To the amazement of the onlookers, the Latta machine was able to get up a head of steam within a few minutes, throw water 225 feet, and throw it through two, four, or six lines of hose at the same time.

The City Council had found what it wanted—the machinery it needed and the excuse it required to tell the volunteers that they must be replaced by "professional" firefighters who could operate the delicate machines. On April 1, 1853, Cincinnati put the first paid fire department in the United States into service. (Cincinnati is popularly known to be the city with the first paid fire department in the United States, but there is evidence that with the employment of a carpenter named Thomas Atkins a few years before, the city of Boston can lay an equal claim to the honor of being first.)

But the volunteers still did not want to give up, and when the new department raced the new steamer to their first fire, the volunteers were waiting for them—vowing that the machine would never operate. This time the volunteers were in for a surprise. Citizens who wanted to protect their new department took the battlers on, and within twenty minutes had routed them.

Two years later, Cincinnati's chief fire engineer was able to report:

FIRST PAID FIRE DEPARTMENT

CINCINNATI
1853

Under the present control the Engine Houses are no longer nurseries where the youth of the city are trained in vice, vulgarity and

Firefighters race to harness the horses at the sound of an alarm.

Above left: New York firefighters pose for a daguerrotype in the 1850s.

Above right: New Orleans volunteer firemen, c. 1855–1860.

Firemark of the Associated Firemen's Insurance Company, Pittsburgh, 1851

VICTORY OF THE STEAM ENGINE

NEW YORK
1855

debauchery, and where licentiousness holds his nightly revels. The Sabbath day is no longer desecrated by the yells and fierce conflicts of rival Fire Companies, who sought the occasion offered by false alarms, often gotten up for the purpose of making brutal assaults upon each other; our citizens, male and female, pass our Engine Houses without being insulted by the coarse vulgarities of the persons collected around them.

In 1855 the Latta Company sent a steam fire engine to the East to demonstrate its abilities. The New York volunteers felt it a point of honor to show that their "masheens" and time-honored traditions could beat the detested steam engine. They confidently put up their most powerful pumper, the Mankiller, to compete with it.

The two engines met in City Hall Park on February 9, 1855. As New York's strongest volunteers waited to begin pumping their big "hay wagon," the three Latta men tinkered with their knobs and gauges and valves and started up their engine. The contest to see which machine could throw water farther and higher was on. The volunteers pumped mightily until, exhausted, they fell off the brakes to be replaced by fresh pumpers. The hoses aimed their water and to the joy of the volunteers, the Mankiller threw it 189 feet while the steamer threw it only 182. A great roar when up and a celebration was on. The volunteers had shown that man and muscle could out-perform a machine.

But could they? Veteran firefighter Zophar Mills and assistant foreman of the Mankiller company John Garside looked at the exhausted volunteers lying near their machine while the steamer pumped on.

"John, that stream stays there," said Mills.

"Yes, it does," replied Garside.

"Well, that settles it," Mills said sadly.

Slowly volunteer companies began to disappear. Unlike the earliest iron steamers that had to be drawn by horses, newer models were made of steel and brass, thus becoming light enough for men to pull them. This consoled the volunteers for a while, since they still could have that job to do. But as cities spread out and distances grew greater, horses again replaced men. And as cities grew, so did the demand for organized paid departments. One by one, major cities converted to steam and to paid, professional firefighters. The colorful day of the volunteers was dying in urban America, although smaller communities would continue to rely on them for fire protection, and they have continued a tradition of dedicated service to this day.

Shortly after the development of the steamer, technology came up with another advance in firefighting—the

Firefighters slide down new poles at the sound of an alarm.

Below: The Latta steam pumper, 1858

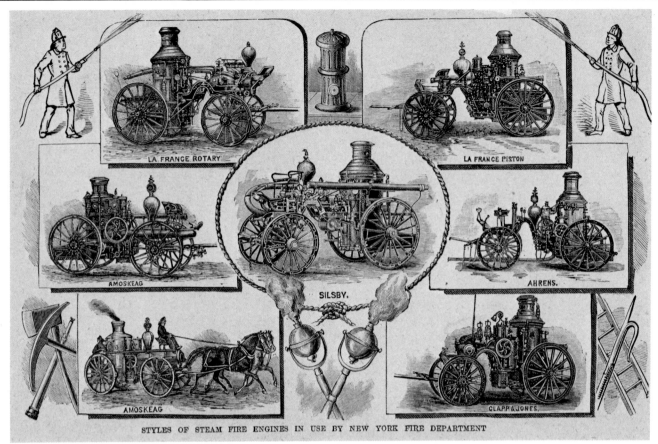

STYLES OF STEAM FIRE ENGINES IN USE BY NEW YORK FIRE DEPARTMENT

Steam fire engines used by the New York City Fire Department, mid 19th century

chemical engine. This vehicle carried two fifty-gallon tanks containing a soda and acid mixture that could be pumped in a strong stream onto a small fire. Because it was so much lighter and more maneuverable than a steamer, the chemical engine could reach a fire scene faster and, with luck, put out the fire before it grew to a size that demanded the use of a steamer.

Speed in responding to a fire, catching it in its earliest stages, is vital to successful firefighting—and that means learning where a fire is in the shortest possible time. For centuries firefighting had depended on a system of bell-ringing to announce a fire and tell firefighters where it was located. But Samuel F. B. Morse's invention of the telegraph in the early 1840s helped to give firefighting a much faster and more accurate alarm system.

A young doctor in Boston, William F. Channing, was also an avid fire buff. Channing saw the possibilities of making telegraphy the servant of firefighting. He designed a system of metal alarm boxes that, when "pulled," would immediately transmit their location to a central office. From here the location of the box would be

FIRST FIRE ALARM BOX SYSTEM

BOSTON
1852

Telegraph apparatus at fire headquarters in New York City

Early fire alarm box

tapped out to firehouses so that the one nearest to the fire alarm box pulled could respond to that location. By 1852 Boston had fire alarm boxes located all over the city, and on April 29 of that year the first fire box alarm was pulled. Other cities were, of course, quick to follow suit, and soon church sextons who had long been roused in the night to ring the alarm could sleep uninterrupted.

To the north of Boston, in Lawrence, Massachusetts, a calamity took place that no fire alarm system could have alleviated. Just as the New York tenement fire in 1860 focused attention on the firefighting problems created by America's growing urbanization, so the tragedy in Lawrence pointed up the problems for firefighters that the nation's growing industrialization was creating.

The scene was the Pemberton Mill, a five-story factory where textiles were produced. According to a resident of Lawrence: "No mill in [this city] was better protected from fire, nor was any mill in the city considered more substantial or secure in any respect. In the opinion of all it was the model mill of the city. It was insured, at the lowest rate at which such property is taken. . . ."

Yet on January 10, 1860, the seemingly impossible happened. At 5:13 in the afternoon, with nearly seven hundred people at work in the main building, it simply collapsed. Five stories filled with workers and textile machinery crashed to the ground. Said the same resident: "Immediately a wail went forth from all beholders, which

COLLAPSE OF THE PEMBERTON MILL

LAWRENCE, MASSACHUSETTS
1860

A building blazes in Boston in 1852 as neighbors watch from nearby roofs.

at a distance, was mistaken for a simultaneous cry of fire. The dust which rose upon the moist still atmosphere from the fallen walls, filling it like a cloud, favored this delusion. The direction, to those at a distance, indicated that a terrible fire had broken out. . . ."

Firefighters were on the scene immediately, helping to dig people out and standing by in case fire should break out. For six hours they, the police, worry-torn relatives and friends, and other able-bodied people struggled to extricate the workers trapped by layers of twisted machinery, wooden beams, and slabs of brick wall.

Then in the darkness of eleven o'clock, one of the rescuers accidentally broke a lantern, and its flames leaped upon the cotton and oil waste in the debris. The fire took hold, slowly at first, but the firefighters were unable to stop it. The streams of water they sent onto it simply washed down and off the collapsed floors like rain off a slanted roof. Soon fire covered the ruins entirely, and there was no longer any hope for those still trapped. They would have to perish in the flames, and at least fourteen of them did.

In all, 88 workers were killed or fatally injured, while another 275 were either badly or slightly injured.

Two days later, an inquest began into the cause of the disaster. Eyewitnesses gave testimony of support columns falling inward and the roof crashing down, setting off a chain reaction moving down floor by floor. The jury concluded that the cast iron columns used in the building's construction had not been strong enough to support the roof, machinery, and flooring because they had not been properly cast, the result of the purchasing agent's attempt to buy the columns a little cheaper per pound.

In 1860 the nation was fast approaching cataclysm. Tensions between North and South grew constantly more strained, and November's Presidential election made the two sections' differences irreconcilable. To the South, Abraham Lincoln and the Republican platform were totally unacceptable, and when the Republicans won, the South made its move. On December 20, 1860, South Carolinians met in convention in their capital at Columbia and voted unanimously to secede from the Union. Seven other southern states quickly followed their lead, and by February 1861 they had formed their own nation —the Confederate States of America.

Mill fire in Fall River, Massachusetts

START OF THE CIVIL WAR

CHARLESTON
1861

WATERFRONT FIRE

CHARLESTON
1861

In the harbor of South Carolina's busy port city of Charleston stood Fort Sumter, manned by federal troops. To southerners it was a symbol of the Union's continuing attempt to hold power over the Confederacy. So, on April 12, 1861, Confederate troops began to bombard the fort from battery implacements in Charleston. Military action had begun, and the Civil War was on.

Fire would again prove a devastating weapon against both sides, whether it was set by accident or by military or civilian design.

Within a year after South Carolina seceded, Charleston suffered a major city fire, a catastrophe that would cause it great suffering during the war against the Union. On December 11, 1861, flames were sighted along the Cooper River on the northern side of the city. Winds of almost hurricane force drove the flames in a southwesterly direction through the heart of Charleston, and they did not stop their destructive rush until they had reached the Ashley River on the southern side of the city. The loss was estimated at a staggering $5 to $7 million ($32.4 to $45.4 million today), and the port city's waterfront was virtually destroyed. The fire severely weakened the city, as did the Union naval blockade that closed off its trade, and the more than three years of siege that rained naval gun shells all over the city. South Carolina was paying dearly for its initiative in secession and war.

Firefighters in the North were quick to answer President Lincoln's call to the colors after the Confederate firing on Fort Sumter, even though they were generally exempted from military service. Within a few days after Fort Sumter's fall, Colonel Elmer E. Ellsworth, a young

Fire Zouaves march into Yorktown.

In a romantic rendering, Zouaves battle flames at Willard's Hotel, Washington, 1861.

friend of Lincoln, arrived in New York to recruit a regiment of fighting men. He went directly to the Fire Department to appeal for brave men to join him. As a contemporary writer put it, "The roll, like a fiery cross, went from engine-house to engine-house, and in three days a regiment of twelve hundred able-bodied men, used to hardship and exposure, was formed."

By April 29, 1861, the First Fire Zouaves, the 11th New York Volunteer Infantry, were ready for action.

Wearing red firemen's shirts, gray jackets, and flowing gray trousers tucked into their boots, the firefighter/soldiers marched through the streets of New York to sail for Washington, D.C., and further orders. The regiment of firefighters was the very first to be formed to meet the challenge to American unity.

On their arrival they were mustered into service on the steps of the Capitol building with President Lincoln in attendance. Thereafter they were billeted in the Capitol, sleeping on its floors. On May 9, the restless Zouaves got word that Willard's, Washington's most prominent hotel, had caught fire. Off to the scene they raced, commandeering firefighting equipment along the way. Within minutes they were vigorously climbing all over the building, putting out fires as they found them. Soon they had "quenched the flames and saved the building, much to the gratification of Mr. Willard, who entertained them at breakfast and gave [them] a purse of $500."

Within two weeks they were ordered to march into the Confederacy and occupy Alexandria, Virginia. Leading his vanguard of Zouaves down Alexandria's streets, Colonel Ellsworth spied a Confederate flag flying from an attic window of the Marshall House hotel. Taking a corporal with him, he mounted the stairs and tore the flag from its pole. Then, wrapping the flag around himself, Ellsworth started back down the stairs. In the main corridor he encountered the proprietor of the hotel, who raised his shotgun and fired.

"My God!" cried Ellsworth as he fell dead.

Ellsworth's corporal immediately fired on his colonel's assailant, in turn killing him, but the Zouaves had lost their first man, and their commander. In two months one hundred more of them would lie dead, casualties of the First Battle of Bull Run.

DRAFT RIOTS

NEW YORK
1863

Not everyone in the North was as anxious to join up as the Fire Zouaves had been. As the war stretched on, there were not enough volunteers to man the Union army, so Congress was forced to initiate a draft system on March 3, 1863. Men were to be chosen by lottery to raise the army up to strength.

In New York City the lottery drawing began peacefully enough, but it soon grew into a four-day orgy of murder, mayhem, and arson—the most brutal and bloodiest riot the nation had ever seen.

Many of those who objected to the draft did so because it was possible for a wealthy man who had three hundred dollars to buy his way out of it. A poorer man, lacking three hundred dollars, had to serve. Many other objectors, though, were simply looking for a fight and a chance to loot, and they were able to mobilize the anti-draft elements into a screaming, destroying mob.

The mob began its work on July 13, 1863, when they demolished the lottery wheel and set fire to the government building that housed it. When firefighters arrived to do their work they were repulsed by the crowd, who wanted to punish the government for the draft. From there mobs roamed the city, breaking into arsenals to take arms and setting fires, again preventing any firefighting attempts to quench them.

Then the mob decided to go after black people, since they blamed them as the cause of the war. Their first target was the Colored Orphan Asylum, which housed two hundred little charges. After first throwing out all bedding and furniture, looting the building, and seizing twenty of the orphans, they set fire to the place. Again firefighters tried to put the fire out, but again the mobs forced them back. Firefighters were, however, able to rescue the captured children and get them to safety.

Draft rioters burn the Colored Orphan Asylum, New York, 1863.

The terror-filled July days of New York's draft riots gave rise to thousands of acts of courage on the part of firefighters. But perhaps most visible of all were those performed by the city's fire chief, John Decker.

CHIEF ENGINEER JOHN DECKER
NEW YORK FIRE DEPARTMENT

A powerful and popular man who had been born next to a firehouse, Decker had become chief when he was only thirty-six years old. Now, nearly four years later, he had maintained his department's strength in spite of the war, and had won the loyalty of his men and the respect of the citizens he served. (As he recalled many years later, "I weighed one hundred and ninety pounds then, and was a safe man to let alone. I could hold my own with the best of them, and that is no mean boast.")

When the draft riot mobs set fire to the first government building, Chief Decker rushed to the scene to direct operations against it. There he faced the shouts and threats of the menacing mob. Leaping on top of an engine, he turned to the seething faces: "Fellow citizens, I appeal to your common sense; I will not say a word at present as to the rights of your cause. . . . You came here to do a certain thing. You have done it. Now you ought to be satisfied. All the U.S. property is destroyed. . . . Let us, as firemen, get to work and save the property of innocent men. The men whose houses are burning now are innocent, they have nothing to do with the draft, they are hard-working men like yourselves; now I ask you, will you let us go to work and put out this fire?"

For the moment he had quieted the angry crowd,

From there the mob began to lynch any hapless blacks they found in the streets and set fire to buildings that housed blacks. By the end of the first day, two hundred people were dead and over a quarter of a million dollars in property had been destroyed.

The rioters continued the next day. All over the city, mobs roamed the streets firing and looting. Firefighters raced from burning building to burning building, able to save some, watching others destroyed. Their lives were threatened, their hoses were cut, but still they kept working, through this day and the next.

Finally enough troops reached the city (rushed back from Gettysburg, where they had fought only a week

Mobs lynch blacks during 1863 New York draft riots.

and his firefighters got to work. But the lull was only temporary. The mob wanted more fire and more blood. When the rioters reached the Colored Orphan Asylum, Decker's words were no longer enough, and he had to resort to physical persuasion. Decker sailed into the mob that was forcing entry into the asylum. He grabbed their axes in an attempt to stop them. But a blow from a cart rung knocked him senseless. A contemporary writer described what happened next: "When consciousness returned he found himself in the hands of a half a dozen infuriated rioters, who were firm in their determination to hang him from the nearest tree. That the miscreants meant business and were prepared to execute their threat was made evident by the fact that one of them carried a stout rope which he shook in the face of the partially stunned but undaunted Chief. . . . His nerve and mother wit alone saved him. Turning to the man who was adjusting the rope into a noose, Chief Decker carelessly remarked, drawing his hand suggestively across his neck:

'What good will it do you to hang me? You will only stop my *draft,* not the Government's.'

The pun saved a good and a brave man's life."

before) to restore order. For four days the city had been a battlefield, and now it tried to tally up its losses. At least 1,200 people had lost their lives, about 150 of whom were blacks while the others were police officers, soldiers, and, of course, rioters. Property loss estimates began at $2 million and went as high as $7 million (from $9.5 to $33 million today).

When the reign of terror ended, the *New York Herald* printed its assessment of the work of the city's firefighters: "No class of men are more entitled to praise for heroism and self-sacrifice, as displayed in the recent uprising against the draft ordered by President Lincoln, than the firemen of New York, in extinguishing fires and saving valuable property that would have been destroyed had they not interposed their objections and determined to execute their functions at every hazard. . . . Hundreds of thousands of dollars were placed in jeopardy, and only saved by prompt interference of the firemen."

New York had been threatened by the rioters' fires, but the city had been saved. Several southern cities were not as fortunate. One by one they met destruction as the war inevitably enveloped them.

One of the first to be devastated in General William T. Sherman's inexorable march to the sea was Atlanta, Georgia. The rail center for the South, this city had been a major supplier of the Confederate troops for more than three years. Northern military strategy called for its destruction. So, on July 20, 1864, General Sherman trained his guns on the city, and the siege began. For more than a month Union cannon shelled Atlanta into submission. Then, on September 2, northern troops occupied the beleaguered city.

For two months the Union forces camped in Atlanta. When they were ready to continue their march to the sea, General Sherman ordered that Atlanta be put to the torch. One of his aides, Major George Ward Nichols, described the scene:

> When the army commenced its southward march Atlanta was given to the flames. On November 15, a grand and awful spectacle is presented with the city now in flames. By order, the chief engineer has destroyed by powder and fire all the storehouses, depot buildings, and machine-shops. The heaven is one expanse of lurid fire; the air is filled with flying, burning cinders; buildings covering two hundred acres are in ruins or in flames; every instant there is the sharp detonation or the smothered booming sound of exploding shells and powder concealed in the buildings, and then the sparks and flame shoot away up into the black and red roof, scattering cinders far and wide. These are the machine-shops where have been forged and cast the rebel cannon, shot and shell that have carried death to many a brave defender of our nation's honor. The warehouses have been the receptacle of munitions of war, stored to be used for our destruction. The city, which, next to Richmond, has furnished more material for prosecuting the war than any other in the South, exists no more as a means of injury to be used by the enemies of the Union.

Leaving a ruined Atlanta behind them, the Union troops moved on toward Savannah. Three days before Christmas, Savannah too fell before the northern forces and submitted to occupation. But the army's stay there would also be relatively short. Sherman had reached the

THE BURNING OF ATLANTA

ATLANTA
1864

Sherman's troops burn McPhersonville, South Carolina, 1865.

sea and now it was time to carve his path of destruction northward. On January 27, 1865, Savannah in its turn was burned to the ground.

Sherman didn't have to stop at Charleston to destroy it by fire. The southerners did that themselves. Confederate troops, evacuating the city, set fire to warehouses containing supplies that approaching Union troops might use. The flames spread to an ammunition dump, which exploded, killing 150 people. Charleston finally surrendered on February 18, 1865.

The Confederacy then turned fire on itself in one more final, desperate act. Richmond, Virginia, the capital of the Confederate States of America, had thus far resisted capture by the North. In 1862 Confederate troops under General Robert E. Lee and General Thomas J. "Stonewall" Jackson had defeated Union forces there and had saved their capital. But now, nearly three years later, the Confederacy recognized that the end was close at hand and Richmond's capture was inevitable. As in Charleston six weeks earlier, Confederate troops set fire to warehouses containing supplies that the Union troops could use. Again the fire got out of hand, due in part to

An early photograph shows the desolation left behind by fire and war in Richmond, 1865.

a high wind and in part to mobs of looters who saw their opportunity. What few firefighters were left in Richmond battled the flames, but, like their New York counterparts in the draft riots, they were thwarted by the mobs. As the northern troops approached Richmond on April 2, 1865, their first job was to fight the fires raging in the city they sought to occupy. By the time they succeeded, nearly all of the central city was destroyed.

Richmond's was the last major fire of the Civil War. One week later the Confederacy surrendered to the Union. The South turned to the job of rebuilding its gutted cities.

The North, with its cities intact and relatively little of its territory battle-scarred, did not have to face the constant and painful reminders of the war that the South did. Proud that the Union had prevailed, northerners could settle back and congratulate themselves on the nation's ninetieth birthday.

In Portland, Maine, a grand celebration of July 4, 1866, was underway. By five o'clock in the afternoon, thousands of people had come in from the surrounding countryside to join the townspeople in watching the evening's promised fireworks display. Small boys raced up and down the streets tossing firecrackers. One of the crackers landed in a pile of wood shavings near a boat-builder's shop, and soon the building was on fire.

JULY 4th FIRE

PORTLAND, MAINE
1866

FIREMAN JOHN DENHAM
NEW YORK FIRE DEPARTMENT

A final fiery postscript to the Civil War was written at Barnum's Museum in New York City three months after the war's end. There the great P.T. himself had set up a diorama of scenes from the war. One scene depicted Confederate President Jefferson Davis attempting to flee Union pursuers, disguised in his wife's petticoats. Southern sympathizers took great offense at this insult to their hero and are thought to have expressed their displeasure by firing Barnum's.

Because the museum also housed wild birds and animals, as well as human freak attractions, the firefighters faced problems in evacuating the building that were vastly different from the usual ones. They had to free the wild birds, who then found themselves flying high above a city they had never seen. A writer of the time described the firefighters' evacuation of the human attractions: "The Fat Lady and the Giantess were handed out in safety with tenderest solicitude for their welfare. Several of the [fire] laddies said they were completely smitten with the woolly-headed Albino woman."

But it was the wild beasts that were the biggest problem, and here Fireman John Denham, "a quiet, retiring sort of fellow" from Hose Company No. 15, came into his own. As the firefighters were trying to release the animals and control them, a huge Bengal tiger freed himself from his cage and came crashing out of a second-story window, landing near the crowd of spectators below. Terror gripped them as the frightened animal advanced. Denham swung into action. Grabbing his axe, he pounced on the beast and with one blow put the big Bengal out of commission. It was Denham's moment in the sun. He never surfaced again as a fire hero, but he had acted with great courage on that July day.

Barnum's Museum fire, 1865

An eyewitness described the crowd's reaction when the fire bell sounded: "No alarm was felt; we had been so greatly favored, that we had grown boastful and presumptuous. Our largest fires had always been so well managed, our fire companies were so zealous and faithful. . . . For the first half hour, indeed, so little concern was felt that very few among the thirty odd thousand inhabitants of our prosperous and beautiful city . . . took the trouble of ascertaining for themselves what the danger was, or which way the wind blew."

But soon they would be all too aware of the wind:

By and by the wind sprang up; a great roaring was heard afar off, and coming nearer and nearer—the door-steps and house-tops began to be crowded with breathless listeners—all conversation was carried on in a low voice, and consisted of little more than brief hurried questions and answers; the heavens gathered blackness, and a hurricane of fire swept over the city, carrying cinders and blazing fragments of wood far into the country. . . .

On swept the whirlwind of fire, spreading out like a fan as it went, directly through the wealthiest and busiest part of our city; and with such inconceivable swiftness, that people knew not whither to fly for safety, and household furniture and costly merchandise had to be moved again and again, only to be burned up at last; and fire-proof warehouses, with iron shutters and slated roofs, crumbled and fell in heaps before the terrific heat. Masses of iron melted—even a mortar used for a sign to an apothecary's shop, on being struck by the fiery blast, fell upon the pavement, like melted lead. Kegs of nails were fused into solid masses, and glass and crockery into jewels, that seem to be greatly prized by the curious, as relics.

The fire department—eighty-five men, four steamers, and one hook and ladder company—fought to contain the blaze. Fire companies from towns and cities in the area rushed to Portland's aid:

Our fire department was admirable . . . and the behavior of our fire companies, worthy of the highest praise from first to last; many of them leaving all they had on earth to be destroyed, or pillaged, while they occupied the fore front of the battle ground—acquitting themselves like men, together with the brave, generous fellows from out of town. But from the first, or within two hours, at furthest, it was seen that steamers and fire companies, however efficient, on all ordinary occasions, were entirely powerless, within the immediate range of the Destroyer. . . .

The fire raged on for twelve hours, burning out half the population and destroying 320 acres at a loss of $10 million to $12 million ($40–$47.7 million today). Only two lives were lost, supposedly those of a pair of citizens who had celebrated too liquidly and did not rouse themselves in time to flee.

One of the town's leading citizens described the scene the next day:

> The calamity was really appalling. Going to the point where the fire commenced, I walked over its whole course. . . . It is a wide scene of desolation, dreary, sickening, awful. I have not seen or imagined anything like it since I traversed the streets of Pompeii a dozen years ago. At the first glance the whole city seemed to be destroyed. There is literally a forest of chimneys, and over the whole region almost the silence of the grave.

During the brief period between October 1871 and November 1872 the United States suffered the three worst fires in its history. In all, these devastating conflagrations claimed more than 1500 lives, destroyed nearly a million and a half acres, and caused $280 million (nearly $1.4 billion today) in damage.

The first of these fires nearly burned down the city of Chicago. A fast-growing prairie settlement, Chicago had a population of 334,000 (seventy times the number it had had thirty years earlier). Although many of its larger and more important buildings were sturdily constructed of iron and stone, thousands more—factories, stores, boarding houses, private homes, barns—were built of wood. Wooden pavement covered 56 miles of its streets, and 651 miles of wooden sidewalks lined its streets and roads.

Rain had not favored Chicago much for three months. Only a few showers had fallen in that time, and the city's acres and acres of wood were bone dry, a fact attested to by the numerous fires that had sprung up recently all over the city. The worst of these—indeed Chicago's worst fire to date—occurred on Saturday night, October 7, 1871. For fifteen hours it burned, as half of Chicago's 185-man force of firefighters battled it. By Sunday morning it had burnt out twenty acres of the city's West Side at a cost of nearly a million dollars. It had also destroyed at least one steamer and one hose cart, injured thirty firefighters, and thoroughly exhausted half of the city's fire department.

So, when fire was again spotted at about eight thirty that Sunday evening, the scene was set for devastation. To add to Chicago's woes, a hard wind was blowing that

THE GREAT CHICAGO FIRE
CHICAGO
1871

Chicagoans flee across bridges as city burns, 1871.

night which fanned the fire's spread. Also, through an unfortunate series of mistakes and mishaps the firefighters were directed time and again to the wrong location. Not until the fire had been raging forty-five minutes to an hour did the first fire company reach it—a circumstance that probably caused the firefight to be over before it started.

The fire had begun in a barn behind the frame house that Kate and Patrick O'Leary owned. Whether, as legend would have it, a cow, angry at being milked by Mrs. O'Leary at this late hour, had kicked over a kerosene lantern (a contention Kate vehemently denied) or whether the fire had a different origin, it spread quickly toward the north and northeast. By the time firefighters finally arrived, thirty buildings were in flames.

As the heat grew more and more intense, it combined with the wind to create convection whirls, or "fire devils."

GEORGE ARMSTRONG

CHICAGO FIRE DEPARTMENT

For many of the men who fought the Chicago fire, the sense of their own physical peril was probably eclipsed by their worry over the families they had left behind them. As they worked relentlessly along with their companies, they must have found it terribly painful not to know the fate of their wives and children.

One such man was a young firefighter named George Armstrong. Having worked for many weary hours battling the blaze, he learned that the fire had now reached Randolph Street and was moving rapidly along the houses there. In one of them were his wife and his new child, born only that morning. He felt that he had to go there and protect them.

As he raced up Randolph, he saw that the lower part of his house was afire. In an upper window he could see his wife Jennie and the baby he had seen only once before. Screaming for a ladder, he dashed for the house. Miraculously, a ladder appeared and he sprang up its rungs. The flames leaping out from the house set the ladder on fire, and so a longer ladder was brought and put against the rapidly burning building. Deftly he swung onto it, sending the burning ladder crashing to the ground beneath him. Within seconds he reached the eaves and called out.

"Jennie, darling, come up quickly. You will be safe here."

But Jennie had fainted when she heard the ladder crash down, thinking that her husband had gone to his death with it. Now, hearing his voice from the dimness, she thought they all were dead. Somehow, though, she struggled toward his voice, and mercifully found herself out in the air and in her husband's arms.

Giving him the baby, she said, "We can die together, George. Thank God for that."

Luckily, at that moment a stream of water struck them, cooling them from the murderous heat of the fire, and making it possible for another firefighter to get them down past the cracking window panes and the treacherous leaping flames.

These little whirlwinds picked up pieces of flaming debris and embers, and transported them to other places where they could start still more fires. Soon overworked firefighters were forced to spread themselves and their equipment even thinner as they raced from fire to fire.

Frightened citizens were rushing out of their homes, trying to get themselves and whatever property they could carry to safety. To the east, across the Chicago River, people were still calm, feeling that the flames could not leap the south branch of the river. But the flames quickly proved them wrong. By two o'clock in the morning these people too were rushing for bridges to cross to flee the flames. The streets were pandemonium. Soon seventy-six thousand Chicagoans would be in flight.

A young Chicago clerk, who at first had raced to the fire out of curiosity, promptly found himself racing away from it out of fear. Along with a terrified crowd, he reached the Court House and City Hall, a building thought to be impervious to fire. Here is how he described what he saw and heard:

> [The building was] surmounted by a cupola in which was hung a large bell. The interior of the building was burning and the flames being carried up through the open space had set the bell to ringing. Above all the sounds of the roaring fire, the wind, and the excited shouts of a moving mass of people, the bell whirled on its frame and over its staunchions, ringing out with a weirdness and a despairing clangorous volume, as though it were possessed of sense and were agonizing in its struggle against destruction. For many years thereafter the memory of its clangor often awoke me at night to recall the scene.
>
> The east and west wings of the Court House were constructed of Joliet limestone—the west wing being the City Hall. I watched for some moments, with a fascination which only the growing danger to myself drew me away from, the effect of the fire upon the city hall. The strong southwest wind was driving the heat in sheets of flame from the hundreds of burning buildings to the west upon the southwest corner of the building with such terrific effect that the limestone was melting and was running down the face of the building with first a slow, then an accelerating movement as if it were a thin white paste.

By seven o'clock in the morning the fire had reached the waterworks, knocking out the pumps. With no water running through the mains and the cisterns dried up, Chicago's firefighters had little ammunition. Fire companies came pouring in from other towns and cities—from as far north as Milwaukee and as far east as Cincinnati—but there was little they could contribute without water. The fire raged relentlessly on, mile after mile. Only a rain could stop the fire before it destroyed the entire city.

Providentially it seemed, at about eleven o'clock Monday evening, more than twenty-six hours after the fire began in O'Leary's barn, the prayed-for rain began to fall. By about three o'clock Tuesday morning, the fire finally died out. Behind it lay a blackened area nearly five miles long and one mile wide. In the rubble lay the bodies of as many as three hundred people; the number was never certain since the flames and heat were so intense that they consumed all remains of many victims—even their bones. One third of the city—17,450 buildings—was in total ruin. Some areas resembled a forest of wall

Fire drives the inhabitants of Peshtigo, Wisconsin, into river, 1871.

fragments, other were completely leveled. People wandered hollow-eyed through the ruins, searching for loved ones, lost property, and shelter.

Estimates of property losses reached a staggering $200 million (nearly $1 billion today), less than half of which was insured. And only $40 million of the insurance was ever paid off, as no fewer than sixty insurance companies went bankrupt. For a while at least, proud Chicago, the "Gem of the Prairie," the "Queen City," looked as though her best days were behind her.

In what has surely been the major coincidence in the history of firefighting, on the very same night at almost the very same hour that the Chicago fire started, another even more deadly fire crackled to life about 250 miles north of Chicago in the small Wisconsin town of Peshtigo.

Located in the lush pine forests of the North Woods, Peshtigo, with its population of about two thousand, was

WISCONSIN FOREST FIRE

PESHTIGO
1871

the center of the area's lumbering industry. There a wealthy Chicago businessman had established a sawmill that cut a daily average of 150,000 feet of lumber, a great deal of which was shipped down to Chicago (where, this same night, it would provide tinder for that city's fire). Across the Peshtigo River, which bisected the town, was an immense woodenware factory. There thousands of wooden objects—buckets, tubs, broom handles, clothespins, barrels, and so on—were turned out daily. The surrounding forests seemed boundless, and therefore so did the town's future.

But on the night of October 8, 1871, the Peshtigo area was suffering from two pieces of bad luck that would also bring Chicago to disaster. It had barely rained at all on that part of Wisconsin since July, and as in Chicago, a great wind was blowing from the southwest. Due to the dryness of the soil and the trees, fires had been springing up in the forest at an increasing rate for the past several days. Indeed, the air around Peshtigo was so smoky that it caused citizens' eyes to water. The previous day a local news correspondent had said, "Unless we have rain soon, a conflagration may destroy this town."

At about nine thirty Sunday night a red glow in the distance signaled still another fire in the forest. Soon the people of Peshtigo heard "a low, moaning, faroff roaring of the wind." Then the roar grew louder, and "a crashing and deep booming" sounded from the woods around the town as fiery trees fell to the forest floor. A Peshtigo historian described what happened then:

> . . . In less than five minutes there was fire everywhere. The atmosphere quickly grew unbearably warm and the town was enveloped by a rush of air as hot as though it were issuing from a blast furnace. The wind lifted the roofs off houses, toppled chimneys and showered the town with hot sand and live coals. The cries of the men, women, and children were scarcely audible above the rumble of exploding gas and crashing timber. People were numb with terror, seeing nothing but fire overhead and all around them.

Firefighting efforts availed nothing in this great firestorm. Peshtigo's only piece of equipment, a hand-drawn pumper, was quickly out of commission, and the hastily formed bucket brigades had to flee before the onrushing flames.

In their panic people ran in all directions to try to escape. Some ran toward the bridge to get to the other side of town. On the bridge they were stopped by people

Prairie fires were a constant threat in the 19th century, and farmers plowed wide swaths around their land to discourage the spread of flames.

with the same idea, crossing from the opposite side. The wooden bridge soon caught fire, sending the people on it over the side and into the river. About forty people ran to a huge boarding house, thinking for some reason that they would be safe there. They were wrong; within a short time all that remained of them and it were ashes. Still other people raced into the river, immersing themselves in the now warm water as the fire burned on, raining sparks and burning debris on their heads. The luckiest ones were those 150 who made it to a low marshy area on the east bank of the river. It did not catch fire, and by clinging to the wet ground they escaped danger.

Within an hour every building in Peshtigo was destroyed, with the exception of one under construction. The greenness of the wood used in it had somehow saved it.

The fire roared on, destroying everything in its path —four hundred farms and several other towns. Finally,

Horses pull steamer to a fire in Boston, 1867.

twenty-four hours after the flames had reached Peshtigo, rain began to fall, as it would begin to fall in Chicago a few hours later. The flames finally succumbed.

The full day of fire had burnt out well over one million acres. An area twenty miles from east to west and sixty miles from north to south was swept clean. An estimated twelve hundred people had been killed (four times as many as in Chicago)—from six hundred to eight hundred in Peshtigo, two hundred on their isolated farms, and the rest in neighboring towns.

In contrast to Chicago, whose plight had been telegraphed immediately all over the nation, news of Peshtigo was long in getting out. It was not until October 10 that word of Peshtigo's devastation reached even as far as Wisconsin's state capital at Madison. There the governor and his staff were organizing relief trains to be sent to Chicago. Hearing of Peshtigo's disaster, the governor hurriedly ordered the trains sent northward instead of southward. Four thousand people were destitute in the North Woods, and they needed help every bit as much as their unfortunate brothers and sisters in Chicago.

THE GREAT FIRE OF BOSTON

BOSTON
1872

The third in the trio of history-making fires in 1871–72 struck Boston on a pleasant autumn day. Unlike Chicago and Peshtigo a year earlier, Boston was suffering

Firefighters try to save Old South Church during 1872 fire in
Boston.

neither drought nor strong wind. But it had a problem all its own. Many of the ninety-three horses the Boston fire department used to pull its heavy steamers and other equipment were all down with equine influenza. So were almost all the other horses in Boston.

Fire horses were a necessary and well-loved part of a firefighting team. They were trained so that at the sound of the firehouse gong they would leave their stalls and run immediately to their proper places in front of the equipment. Harness hung above them, and with a turn of a lever it would be dropped down on their waiting and properly positioned backs. With a few adjustments, they were ready to race the heavy machinery to a fire.

But not this day, not in Boston. Instead many of them lay in their stalls weak, cold, and swollen, unable to rouse themselves for any cause. The firefighters themselves then had to struggle to pull their heavy engines through Boston's narrow, winding streets, delaying their arrival at the fire.

At about seven thirty on Saturday evening, November 9, 1872, fire alarms began sounding. A six-story granite building in the city's weekend-deserted commercial section was ablaze. It had been discovered by the men of Engine Company No. 7, who immediately went to work on it. Unfortunately, though, they did not turn in an alarm to fire headquarters. Therefore, as one contemporary writer put it, "The largest portion of the department was first notified [of the fire] by the brilliant pyrotechnic display which illuminated the entire city." Within only fifteen minutes of the fire's discovery it had "assumed fearful proportions."

When other firefighters did finally reach the fire scene, an impossible task faced them: ". . . The heat was so intense that it was extremely dangerous to locate any piece of apparatus within a hundred feet of the actual seat of fire. . . . So intense was the heat that the stone coping of the building sixty feet distant from the fire began to burst and crumble. . . . So rapid was the spread of fire that at the moment of giving the alarm, six other equally large granite buildings were enveloped in flames, and the building where it originated was a roaring furnace."

Boston's Chief John S. Damrell sent out a call for help from neighboring communities, as he and his men worked on to try to stop the fire's spread. But then the water supply failed. Chief Damrell had long before warned City Hall that the four-inch mains would not

Membership Certificate of the Newton, Massachusetts, Hose Company No. 6. Illustrations are scenes from Currier & Ives lithographs. (Insurance Company of North America)

Rival New York companies, one pulling hand
pumper and the other a spider-type hose reel, race to
a fire in an 1854 lithograph by Currier entitled
"The Race—'Jump her boys, jump her!'"

Right: Parade hat from Biddeford, Maine, 1860s.

(Insurance Company of North America)

Upper left: Engine panel from Americus No. 6 Company, New York, 1849, shows Psyche being carried off to Olympus.

Lower left: "Prompt to the Rescue," lithograph by Currier & Ives, 1858.

Above: Engine panel from Lexington No. 7 Company, New York, 1849, depicts the battle of Lexington, 1775.

(Insurance Company of North America)

Firefighters fill their steam pumper from a handy stream in this mid-nineteenth-century lithograph.
(Culver Pictures)

Below: Both steam and hand pumpers are used by firefighters in 1858 Currier & Ives lithograph entitled "Facing the Enemy."
(Insurance Company of North America)

Diligent Hose Company of Philadelphia's 1871 membership certificate features the Hose House embellished with firemen in working (left) and parade (right) dress.
(Insurance Company of North America)

Below: Fire destroys Chicago, 1871.
(The Bettmann Archive)

Horse-drawn steamer, hose-reel cart, and hook and ladder rush to a New York fire in 1866
Currier & Ives lithograph. (Insurance Company of North America)

Trappers fight prairie fire with fire in 1862 Currier & Ives lithograph.
(Picture Collection, New York Public Library)

Below: Mid-nineteenth-century painting shows gleaming steamer.
(The Bettmann Archive)

Firefighters battle theater blaze as bystanders watch, Cincinnati, 1850. (Picture Collection, New York Public Library)

WILLIAM FARRY DANIEL COCHRAN   JOHN CONNELLY

Attempts to rescue people trapped by fire are commonplace in a firefighter's work, but the courage that many of these attempts require is anything but commonplace.

At about seven o'clock that Sunday morning, as the Boston fire continued to blaze away, two men, thought at the time to be employees of the Weeks & Potter store, were madly trying to salvage goods from their burning building. They heard a sickening rumble, and then saw part of the side wall crashing down toward them. One of the men was buried completely, but the other found that only his legs were pinned. Crying for help, he screamed that if only someone would free his legs, he would be safe.

A contemporary writer described what happened then:

Several firemen responded by dashing into the doomed building, the front wall of which was even then tottering, and making frantic efforts to release the poor fellow. Suddenly they were startled by a cry that the massive front wall behind them was going over. There was a desperate rush for life, and a silent horror seized the spectators as the wall fell with a thundering crash and it seemed that two of the firemen had shared the fate of those whom they had tried to save.

The two brave firefighters had indeed shared that fate. Foreman William Farry and Assistant Foreman Daniel Cochran of Boston's Hook and Ladder Company No. 4 lay dead in the rubble. Dead along with them was the man they had risked their lives to free. It turned out that he too was a firefighter, John Connelly of West Roxbury's Hook and Ladder Company No 1.

Boston firefighters carry hose into burning house.

provide sufficient water in a real emergency, and this was just that emergency.

A historian of Boston's fire department described what happened next:

The fire raged for eighteen hours with relentless fury. The streets became veritable blow-pipes, by reason of their narrowness and the height of the buildings upon them, causing such intense heat that blocks of granite stores would melt, as it were, and fall before the flames had approached within five hundred feet of them. At last, the working force had been so augmented by the reënforcements from out of town that the adequate supply of water from the tide reservoirs along the southern, eastern, and northern boundaries of the fire could be made available, and at 3 o'clock in the morning a continuous line of battle was formed. . . . This line embraced forty-two steam engines, which advanced with an ardor and pluck that evinced their determination to stop and conquer further devastation. The work here performed demanded and evoked the commendation and admiration of those competent to judge of its efficacy, and by it the flames were driven to a common centre, the army holding every point gained in the attack.

When the fire was finally brought under control early Sunday afternoon, the people of Boston could survey their losses. Thirteen people were dead—nine of them firefighters. One square mile of the city's richest section—776 buildings—was destroyed, and losses were estimated at $75 million ($364.6 million today). In the long history of Boston's city fires, this had clearly been the worst.

Four years after the Boston fire, another fire was to enter America's "worst to date" annals—this time it was the worst theater fire.

Theaters had always been potentially dangerous to life in case of fire. The enclosure in a fairly small place of a large number of people forced to rely on a limited number of stairways and exit doors seemed to invite disaster —and it often did.

On the evening of December 5, 1876, one thousand people had gone to the Brooklyn Theatre in Brooklyn, New York, to see the popular melodrama *Two Orphans.* At about 11:15, as the final act was drawing to a close, Miss Kate Claxton, the leading actress, lay on a straw pallet. Mr. Henry Murdoch, her leading man, was delivering a speech when they both heard whispers of "Fire" from backstage. Looking up, they spotted the flames, still not visible to the audience, above them in the flies. Mr. Murdoch faltered, but Miss Claxton prodded him.

"Go on," she whispered, "they will put it out, there will be a panic—go on."

As carpenters behind the scenes tried to beat the fire out, the actors went valiantly on with their lines. But the audience was soon aware that something was very wrong. A great murmuring swept the hall and people began rising from their seats. The four actors onstage then gave up all pretense of the play and sought to calm the crowd. One pleaded:

THE
BROOKLYN
THEATRE FIRE

NEW YORK
1876

The balcony collapses as fire rages in the Brooklyn Theatre, 1878.

"Ladies and gentlemen, there will be no more play, of course; you can all go out if you will only keep quiet."

Joining hands with her fellow actors onstage, Miss Claxton added coolly, "We are between you and the flames."

For a while the audience remained calm and exited in orderly and efficient manner. But as the flames grew, so did the fears of those high up in the gallery, those who would have a long way to go before they could get out. Panic seized the crowd, and the rush was on.

A witness described the scene:

> The exit from the first balcony was down a single flight of stairs in the rear of the vestibule. Down these stairs the people came in scores, leaping and jumping in wild confusion. The way out from the

upper gallery was down a short flight of stairs starting from the south wall of the building, thence by a short turn down a long flight against the same wall to the level of the balcony, and from this floor down a cased flight into Washington Street. The main floor and first balcony were soon emptied through their respective exits, but for the five or six hundred panic-stricken gallery spectators to pass safely through the tortuous passage described was next to an impossibility. Every indication points to the fact that, suffocated by the smoke forced down like a wall from the roof, the mass of those in the upper gallery thronged about the entrance to the stairs, and were either blocked there so as to make exit impossible, or were unable even to make the attempt to escape, and sank down, one upon the other, to fall in a mass into the horrible pit under the vestibule when the supports of the gallery were burned away.

Within fifteen minutes the theater was engulfed in fire. Within thirty minutes the roof had fallen and the broad east wall had crashed inward.

On the morning of December 6, firefighters who had worked so hard to regain order among the frightened audience and lead them to safety found how unsuccessful they had been. Nearly three hundred people, mostly from the upper gallery, had been killed, the victims of their own panic and an inadequate exit system. More than a hundred of the bodies were beyond identification, so a huge common grave was dug for them at Greenwood Cemetery and a mass funeral held.

It was too late for these people, but their misfortune prompted the enactment of stricter fire laws concerning the size and number of exits from theaters in New York. Once again it had taken a major tragedy to bring about better fire protection.

Watchman raises fire signal on a church balcony in Charleston, South Carolina, 1870s.

Fire company membership certificates became increasingly ornate as the 19th century progressed.

The 1870s was unquestionably one of the nation's most disastrous decades for fires. Each tragic fire renewed the awareness among Americans of the terrible dangers of fire, and illustrated the great need for rethinking and re-defining the defenses against future conflagrations. Consequently the 1870s also became a time of innovation, and several important advances in firefighting equipment were made.

Among the first was the Skinner hose elevator—a machine that could raise a platform in a telescoping manner to a height of about fifty feet. The rider of this rather shaky platform could then train a stream of water into a building's upper stories. Chicago had taken delivery on one of these machines a year before the great 1871 fire, and it saw service there as Hose Elevator No. 1. (In the 1880s a water tower came into operation that could be directed from below. No longer was it necessary for a firefighter to make a perilous ascent to train the hose on flames. Now the stream could be directed from the ground.)

AMERICA'S FIRST STEAM FIREBOAT

BOSTON
1873

Both the Chicago and the Boston fires pointed up the need to be able to fight waterfront fires from the water itself. The idea of fireboats was by no means a new one. New York had tried it as far back as 1809 with a wooden whaleboat that held a hand pumper. Twenty-four strong and hearty crewmen were needed to row it through often rough and treacherous waters to a fire scene, where six more men were needed to pump it. Called a "floating engine," it proved too difficult to maneuver and by 1824 New York had abandoned it.

But now, fifty years later, with the advent of steam power, Boston's Chief Damrell thought the fireboat was an idea whose time had come. In 1873 Boston's fire department put a seventy-five-foot iron-hulled fireboat into service. A steam tug, it was fitted with fire engine machinery built by Amoskeag, the highly respected manufacturer of steam fire equipment. The power of this machinery was equal to that of four first-class fire engines, and it could play eight streams of water at one time. Soon every major waterfront city was ordering fireboats.

The next year saw the invention of the first practical sprinkler system. Henry Parmelee, a manufacturer of pianos, had long feared what fire could do to the fine

An early fireboat, the *William. F. Havemeyer,* New York

The Babcock self-acting fire engine on trial before the board of fire commissioners, New York, 1870s

instruments being built in his factory. He hit upon the idea of lining his ceilings with a series of water pipes into which he had inserted valves plugged by pieces of metal that would melt at 155°F. Thus if fire started in the factory, the heat would melt the plug and water would spray all over the area.

In that same year of 1874, Amoskeag ran an advertisement for one of its new steamers: "The propelling and steering apparatus are very simple in this construction, and are so arranged as not to interfere in the least with the use of ordinary drawing for either horses or men, if it is desirable to use them. The propelling is done by the same wagons that are used for the pumps and these are made reversible, so that the machine can be propelled backwards and forwards, as desired."

Like the fireboat, the idea for a self-propelled rather than horse-drawn engine had been around for a long time, but only now was technology making it more feasible. First the volunteers had been replaced by the horses. Now it was becoming more possible to replace the horses as well.

One of the most enthusiastic, skillful, and daring firefighters to use the Skinner was Phelim O'Toole of the St. Louis Fire

Department. As he had gone to sea when he was little more than a boy, "where he learned to hang at dizzy heights by almost imperceptible supports," the Skinner's shaky ladder held no terror for him—a lucky break, it turned out, for guests who were stopping at St. Louis's Southern Hotel the night of April 17, 1877.

Shortly after midnight an alarm came in announcing that the Southern Hotel was afire. Within minutes O'Toole and his Skinner were at the scene, and he was racing up the ladder toward four people hanging out of an upper window. O'Toole described what happened next:

When I got to the top of the fly-ladder I was still about five feet below the window in which the people were. My rope I couldn't pass up. . . . I shouted to one of them, "You pass me a sheet." "What do you want with it?" said he. "You pass it down and I'll save your lives." So I got the sheet and twisted it, and then went into the window where they were, on it, I made a life preserver fast to the centerpiece of the window. I made fast to Mr. Rees and lowered him down on the window-sill under me. . . . I then sent his wife down, and he shoved her out to the ladder, where she was caught and pulled on by a fireman. Next I sent a light woman, Joanna Halpin, down, and Mr. Rees wanted to catch her and shove her over to the ladder like he had done his wife, and I swore at him in a way that I oughtn't to have done. So he let go of her and I dropped her down onto the porch below, where she was easily taken off. I hauled up the rope again and sent down this girl, Burke, a big, heavy woman. I thought she weighed 200 on the end of that line.

One of the problems that had constantly bedeviled firefighters was their inability to reach the high floors and rooftops of burning buildings, either to fight a fire or to save people who were trapped by it. Ladders that could reach sixty-five or seventy-five feet were available, but they were extremely heavy, difficult to position, and unsteady—firefighters were understandably wary of them.

In San Francisco, Daniel D. Hayes, the fire department's superintendent of steamers, began to work on the problem. By 1870 he was able to patent his "Hayes Hook & Ladder and Fire Escape Combined." This rig was able to carry an eighty-five-foot aerial ladder to a fire scene, and there four men could crank it up to its full height.

The rope got foul of Rees and his sheet, and so I says to myself, "Old gal, it ain't going to hurt you to drop the rest of the way." So I let her go by the run, about four or five feet, and she landed alright. . . . It was getting pretty hot and smoky, but I did my best. Then we moved to another window and got two women and a man out the same way. Not a living soul was then to be seen. We saved everybody that showed their face and so we got around to Elm street.

On Elm Street, O'Toole saved the lives of five more people, making a total of twelve that night. Within only three years he would lose his own life, at the age of thirty-two. He rode his beloved Skinner for the last time as it bore him to his grave.

Firefighters rescue guests from the burning Southern Hotel in St. Louis, 1877.

Skepticism about Hayes's "big stick" was rife for the first few years, but soon he was getting orders for his well-designed and well-made "truck" from all over the country. In 1882 the LaFrance Fire Engine Company bought Hayes's patents and by the end of the century, 290 of these aerial ladders were in use.

At this same time firefighter Chris Hoell of the St. Louis fire department came up with a different idea for reaching upper stories; he designed what he called a scaling ladder, one that could be used to climb up the outside of a building. Hoell's ladder consisted simply of a center rod about eight feet long on which crossbars were positioned at intervals of about nine inches. At the top, at

WILLIAM H. NASH

CHIEF OF FOURTH BATTALION
HOOK AND LADDER COMPANY NO. 6

PHILIP MAUS
WILLIAM HUGHES

ENGINE COMPANY NO. 9
FIRE DEPARTMENT OF NEW YORK

Part of the skepticism about the safety of aerial ladders resulted from a demonstration in New York that ended in tragedy.

At the same time Daniel Hayes was developing his aerial ladder in San Francisco, an Italian inventor, Paulo Porto, was also developing a model. It came in several sections and was also raised by cranks and cog wheels. In 1873 Mrs. Mary Bell Scott-Uda, who was in charge of the American rights to Porto's ladder, talked New York's Fire Department into testing it. The test was successful, and the city ordered three of the aerials.

On September 14, 1875, a public demonstration was planned for one of the new Scott-Uda ladders. Eight firefighters from various companies were selected to ascend the ladder as it was extended to its full height of ninety-eight feet. At about eleven o'clock in the morning, Battalion Chief William H. Nash gave the order to ascend. At first the men seemed uneasy, but the brave Nash,

Extension ladder demonstration, New York, 1861

who had already climbed to the top of the ladder once that morning, encouraged them.

"Why, there's no danger," he exclaimed as he started nimbly up the rungs.

With that the men started up behind him at intervals of about ten feet, and in short order Nash had reached the top and Philip Maus and William Hughes had reached the third section.

But then a shriek went up from the crowd. The ladder had begun swaying back and forth dangerously.

"Come down," shouted the Chief of the Fire Department.

White-lipped and trembling, the men eagerly began to obey his order.

Too soon, though, a loud snap announced that all of them would not make it safely. The third section had broken off, plunging the top three men to their deaths.

As the city mourned the dead firefighters, rumors of a scandal began to circulate. It was reported that the chief of the board of fire commissioners had demanded a kickback on the sale of the ladders to the city. In order to pay the kickback and still make a profit, the manufacturers had made the ladders of inferior wood and had constructed them shoddily.

The commissioner was dismissed, but his greed had killed three brave firefighters, a memory that was hard to erase. It would be more than ten years before New York's firefighters would again risk their lives on an aerial ladder.

right angles with the crossbars, was a hook of a size that would fit over a windowsill. To use the scaling ladder, a firefighter would raise it to the window of the story above him, hook it over the sill (breaking through the window, if necessary), and climb up. Once he reached that window, he would repeat the process, and in this manner scale as many stories as necessary, going higher than any ladder—conventional or aerial—could reach. The firefighter, once having attained the necessary height, could then assist a victim down the ladder to the floor below the fire, or, by reversing the climbing process, all the way down to street level. Fireman Hoell's invention made it possible to rescue countless people who otherwise would have been beyond the firefighter's grasp.

Firefighters using Hoell scaling ladder

The West was the land of opportunity in these days, and it was not uncommon for a western town to increase more than tenfold in population in a matter of a decade. Such a place was Seattle, Washington, in 1889.

Seattle resembled every other American city in its infancy—narrow streets, frame buildings, and insufficient fire protection. And like such cities before it—Boston, New York, New Orleans, Pittsburgh—it was bound to be attacked by fire in a major way.

At about 2:15 in the afternoon of June 6, 1889, a pot of glue boiled over on a hot stove in a cabinet maker's shop. As the burning glue hit the floor, the wood shavings there burst into flame. Workers tried to put the fire out by means of a bucket brigade, but in no time it sent them scurrying out of the building and into the street. The curious seemed more intent on watching the flames than on reporting the fire, and it was half an hour before anyone thought to sound the alarm.

Two or three minutes after that the nearest firefighters arrived with a steamer and a hose cart, but by now the smoke was so thick that they did not know where to train the water. Blindly they sent the stream into the mountains of smoke, but the fire was already out of control.

Nevertheless the firefighters carried on, valiantly battling the blaze with their meager equipment—two engines and two hoses—and with a rapidly dwindling water supply that allowed them to send a stream no more than ten feet. At this point the formerly carnival-like crowd turned ugly and began to jeer at the volunteers (like many western cities, Seattle had not yet gone to a paid depart-

GLUE FIRE

SEATTLE
1889

Panic in a frontier village, 1881

ment), blaming them for the fire's rapid progress while at the same time hindering their work.

In one final desperate attempt to contain the roaring inferno, dynamite was brought in to blow up all the buildings in the fire's path. But the effect was exactly the opposite of what was intended—instead of stopping the flames, the explosion merely created a path of kindling down which they could race even faster.

Seattle's call for help from other cities was answered with the speed and generosity typical of firefighting companies. Tacoma firefighters loaded themselves and their equipment on the Northern Pacific and made the run in sixty-three minutes. But by this time, just as had happened in Chicago, the water system had failed, so there was little the additional men could do to stop the fire.

Finally, more than seven hours after the fire began, it simply ran out of anything to destroy and burned itself out. The heart of the city—116 acres, or thirty-one blocks —had been leveled. Seattle's mercantile row was gone, four fifths of a mile. So was "every wharf, warehouse, mill, factory, machine shop and lumber yard . . . the waterfront was nothing but blazing timbers and piles."

Firefighters in Virginia City, Nevada, 1898

New Orleans volunteer George Palmer Holmes poses in full parade dress for photographer in 1880s.

Left: A typical three-horse team rushes to a fire in Chicago in the 1890s.

NIGHT OF TERROR

SPOKANE
1889

DANCE HALL FIRE

CRIPPLE CREEK, COLORADO
1896

The most modest estimate for the losses suffered exceeded $8 million ($50 million today).

Seattle immediately went to work rebuilding its lost structures, its demoralized fire department, and its inadequate fire protection system. It was resolved unanimously that never again would a frame building be constructed in the burnt-out district. The chastened citizens wanted to see that Seattle's sad fate was never repeated.

Spokane, directly across the state of Washington, was experiencing the same kind of growth as Seattle—and it was setting itself up for the same kind of disaster. The parallels between the Seattle fire and the fire that attacked Spokane the following August 4 seem endless. Both had suffered a long dry spell and both had an inadequate water supply. In each, the fire seemed trifling enough at the start, one that might easily be put out by a bucket brigade. But both had roared out of control, the heat creating winds that carried burning embers far afield. A businessman described its intensity as he vainly tried to save his office building: ". . . the heat was so terrific it crumpled the steel shutters up like tissue paper and the brick walls seemed to melt like wax. . . ."

After "a night of terror, devastation and awful woe," Spokane drew a final parallel with Seattle. About the same area was destroyed—thirty-two blocks, the entire business district—and almost the same dollar value was lost—about $6 million. Spokane's fire produced one statistic that Seattle's had not—two persons were killed.

As the two Washington cities rebuilt themselves and continued their growth, far to the south and east a new settlement was just about to make its mark in American history and folklore. In 1891 Cripple Creek was a small Saturday-night town in the cattle-producing center of Colorado. Overnight, though, it turned into a boom town when a cowboy named Bob Womack discovered gold in its hills. A new gold rush was on, and by 1896 Cripple Creek could and did boast twenty-eight millionaires. It could also claim that just one of its blocks harbored twenty-six saloons. Gambling houses and dwellings euphemistically called "dance halls" abounded. So did about eight hundred more conventional businesses.

On Saturday, April 25, 1896, Cripple Creek was getting ready to enjoy the evening when loud voices were heard in a room over the Central Dance Hall. A bartender and one of the "girls" were having an argument that was punctuated with slaps, punches, and—finally—a kicked-over kerosene lamp. As flames spread the fight was forgotten and the man and woman fled.

Within minutes the dance hall was a mass of flames and the residents were clambering out of its windows, sliding down rope escapes when possible, jumping when desperate. The fire raced madly through the neighboring buildings, showing no moral discrimination as it took with it banks and saloons, hardware stores and gambling houses. (One eyewitness told of a survival-minded proprietor who saw that his gambling house was doomed: "Realizing this, the owner had ordered lumber, carpenters, and labor to erect a new building, while the roulette wheels were still turning as the fire approached. All of the gambling equipment was moved out before the fire reached the place and wagons loaded with lumber were waiting on Bennett Avenue between 2nd and 3rd Streets and carpenters with tools were standing by before the place was on fire. The embers were still smoking on the back of the lot when a new building was being started on the hot ground in front and roulette wheels were again turning that night.")

Within three hours, thirty acres of Cripple Creek were in ashes and fifteen hundred people had been burned out. The townsfolk did not know it, but that was just the beginning.

Four days later a grease fire began in the unscathed Portland Hotel. One young boy, seeing the flames, ran to

Cripple Creek, Colorado, after the 1891 fire

HERMAN STAUSS
GEORGE WELLS

HOOK AND LADDER NO. 1
MILWAUKEE FIRE DEPARTMENT

Hotels of the late 1800s were frequently fire-traps, and the Newhall Hotel in Milwaukee, Wisconsin was a perfect example. Six stories high, it lacked both adequate fire escapes and enclosed interior staircases. Unprotected elevator shafts added to the danger, as did the telegraph wires that surrounded the hotel's outer walls.

On the subfreezing night of January 9, 1883, three hundred guests were staying there. At about four o'clock in the morning the sleeping guests were aroused by cries of "Fire!" Panic-stricken, they ran out into the halls only to find them so blackened with smoke that they could not locate whatever exits there were.

Firefighters arrived to find the hotel windows filled with screaming people begging to be rescued. The telegraph wires presented a cruel barrier to rescue. They prevented firefighters from raising their ladders to those trapped, and they entangled those desperate enough to jump.

Herman Stauss and George Wells of Hook and Ladder No. 1 could not bear "the shrieking and calling for help." Racing into an adjoining building, they rigged up a ladder bridge across a twenty-foot alley-way to the hotel's fifth floor, where many of the serving girls were housed. As Wells held the ladder in its precarious position, Stauss crossed it time and again, each time bringing back another girl. In all, the two firefighters saved sixteen of them. But for Stauss's and Wells's courage, the death toll that terrible night would have been eighty-seven instead of a still appalling seventy-one.

Herman Stauss and George Wells rescue woman from the Newhall Hotel in Milwaukee, 1883.

THOMAS J. AHEARN

FIRE DEPARTMENT OF NEW YORK
CAPTAIN

Jacob Riis is probably best remembered as a reformer, a man whose words and pictures forced the American people to recognize the ugliness and horror of slum living around the turn of the century. A man of courage himself, he held a deep admiration for courage in others, especially in firefighters. In February 1898 he published an article entitled "Heroes Who Fight Fire," in which he described the selfless and courageous acts of several firefighters he had watched over the years. One was Chief Thomas J. Ahearn, who had won a medal for bravery for crawling over reservoirs of naphtha as fire raged overhead to drag an unconscious man to safety. One year after that brave deed he nearly lost his life in another rescue attempt. This is how Riis described Ahearn's gallant try at saving a child thought to be trapped in a burning tenement:

Chief Ahearn's quarters were near by, and he was the first on the ground. A desperate man confronted him in the hallway. "My child! my child!" he cried and wrung his hands. "Save him! He is in there." He pointed to the back room. It was black with smoke. In the front room the fire was raging. Crawling on hands and feet, the chief made his way into the room the man had pointed out. He groped under the bed, and in it, but found no child there. Satisfied that it had escaped, he started to return. The smoke had grown so thick that breathing was no longer possible, even at the floor. The chief drew his coat over his head, and made a dash for the hall door. He reached it only to find that the spring-lock had snapped shut. The door-knob burned his hand. The fire burst through from the front room and seared his face. With a last effort, he kicked the lower panel out of the door, and put his head through. And then he knew no more.

His men found him lying so when they came looking for him. The coat was burned off his back, and of his hat only a wire rim remained. He lay ten months in the hospital and came out deaf and wrecked physically. At the age of 45 the board retired him to the quiet of a country district with a commendation for his "brilliant and meritorious services in the discharge of duty which will always serve as an example and an inspiration to our uniformed force."

the nearest fire station. There only one piece of equipment had survived the earlier fire—a hose cart. But even that was not in proper working order; the hose had been wound around the reel backwards, so that the nozzle end was out rather than the fire hydrant end. All one thousand feet had to be turned around. By that time the fire was out of control. Saturday's scene was reenacted, and when the fire finally burned itself out a total of five hundred people were homeless.

But the same optimism that had brought people to Cripple Creek in the first place reasserted itself, and they quickly rebuilt. As long as there was gold in those hills, Cripple Creekers would stick around to get it, one way or another.

WORLD'S COLUMBIAN EXPOSITION

CHICAGO, ILLINOIS 1893

In 1893 Chicago was the proud host to a gigantic World's Fair. Nearly seven hundred acres of the city's lakefront became the site of a "dream city" of the future. Prominent American architects designed what came to be called the "White City," an agglomeration of classical buildings that housed the Fair's myriad exhibitions.

No strictly utilitarian buildings were to mar the beauty and elegance of the White City, so even these structures were dressed up to fit classical lines. A case in point was a cold storage warehouse for the Fair's perishable goods. A wooden structure, it was built around an iron smokestack that connected with a series of boilers. The building was covered with "staff," a kind of plaster that gave the look of stone. The smokestack was enclosed in an elaborate staff-covered wooden tower to disguise its mundane looks and purpose. As one writer put it, "The structure was made for burning," and several times the Exposition's fire department had been called to put out minor fires in the tower, started by sparks escaping from the smokestack.

But one hot July day the tower fire would not be minor. Before it was over, twelve firefighters and eight workmen would be dead. Captain James P. Barry recalled that day twenty-five years later:

The events of the tragic fire at the Cold Storage Warehouse on July 10th are as vivid to me as though they happened yesterday. We had just finished eating our dinner when the box hit. It was 32 minutes after 1 o'clock. When we reached the Cold Storage building, we could see that a tough job was in store for us. At the very top of the tower, which was erected around the chimney extending 116 feet above the roof, a flicker of fire could be seen. We had last been called to this building for the same kind of fire on June 21st and well knew the job to be done. Before

Optimistic late 19th-century advertisement.

Opposite: Ladder and hose truck with chemical extinguisher, c. 1898–1905

Americans entered the twentieth century with all of the exuberance of the eternal optimist. In the last hundred years their nation had grown from a few states along the Atlantic Ocean and a sparsely populated territory extending only as far west as the Mississippi River to what could truly be called an American empire, extending across a continent and into territories beyond.

America's technological wizardry had made a great contribution to this phenomenal growth. So had its rapidly expanding population—five million people in 1800 had become seventy-five million in 1900. Ever-improving technology was now being used to accommodate the ever-growing numbers. Such improvements were making it we could get started, the whole tower at the peak was burning.

I took my company to the roof of the plant by means of the interior wooden stairway. I was ordered to take six men and proceed to the balcony at the 72 foot level of the tower, to assist the Engine companies in hoisting a hose line and 25 foot ladder up the outside of the tower by means of ropes, and operate from that point. The hose was made fast to the balcony and the pipe carried up the ladder to a distance of about 87 feet when the tower quivered and curled up like a match which had burned to the end.

Fire had worked down between the smoke-stack and tower and broken out midway between where we were hanging and the roof. We were cut off completely. Our ropes and the hose line burned through. Some of the men attempted to reach safety by sliding a rope of hose, but they, with the other men on the balcony, fell the 85 foot distance to the roof. Except for myself my company was wiped out.

It is not recorded how Captain Barry was saved from the fate of his comrades.

Firefighters trapped atop the tower of the Cold Storage Warehouse at the Columbian Exposition in Chicago, 1893

JOHN R. VAUGHAN

FIRE DEPARTMENT OF NEW YORK
SERGEANT

In "Heroes Who Fight Fires" Jacob Riis also described the work of Sergeant John R. Vaughan during a hotel fire that claimed many lives. Having narrowly missed death when he first arrived at the fire—a man leaping from a high floor came crashing down within an inch of Vaughan—the intrepid firefighter put his life on the line again and again that early Sunday morning. Seeing that he could not get into the burning hotel, Vaughan raced into the building next door and up its stairs. There across a narrow passage he faced a hotel window from which three men and a woman stared out at him, helpless as the fire closed in on them. Calling to his comrade to hold his leg, Vaughan caught hold of some electric wires dangling from the hotel wall. Trusting that his rubber boots would save him from electrocution, he made a bridge of his body, over which the four trapped hotel guests crawled to safety.

A cry then called Vaughan's attention to another man caught on the hotel's fifth floor with seemingly no hope of escape. Racing to the roof with four of his men, Vaughan faced the man, as Riis said, ". . . only a jump away, but a jump which no mortal might take and live." Here is how Riis described what happened next:

"It is no use," the doomed man said, glancing up. "Don't try. You can't do it."

The sergeant looked wistfully about him. Not a stick or a piece of rope was in sight. Every shred was used below. There was absolutely nothing. "But I couldn't let him," he said to me, months after . . . "I just couldn't, standing there so quiet and brave." To the man he said sharply:

"I want you to do exactly as I tell you, now. Don't grab me, but let me get the first grab." He had noticed that the man wore a heavy overcoat, and already laid his plan.

"Don't try," urged the man. "You cannot save me. I will stay here till it gets too hot; then I will jump."

"No, you won't," from the sergeant, as he lay at full length on the roof, looking over. "It is a pretty hard yard down there. I will get you, or go dead myself."

The four sat on the sergeant's legs as he swung free down to the waist; so he was almost able to reach the man on the window with outstretched hands.

"Now jump—quick!" he commanded; and the man jumped. He caught him by both wrists as directed, and the sergeant got a grip on the collar of his coat.

"Hoist!" he shouted to the four on the roof; and they tugged with their might. The sergeant's body did not move. Bending over till the back creaked, it hung over the edge, a weight of two hundred and three pounds suspended from and holding it down. The cold sweat started upon his men's foreheads as they tried and tried again, without gaining an inch. Blood dripped from Sergeant Vaughan's nostrils and ears. Sixty feet below was the paved courtyard. . . .

To relieve the terrible dead weight that wrenched and tore his muscles, he was swinging the man to and fro like a pendulum. Then it came to him: He could *swing him up!* A smothered shout warned his men. They crept nearer the edge without letting go their grip on him, and watched with staring eyes the human pendulum swing wider and wider, farther and farther, until now, with a mighty effort, it swung within their reach. They caught the skirt of the coat, held on, pulled in, and in a moment lifted him over the edge.

They lay upon the roof, all six, breathless, sightless, their faces turned to the winter sky. . . . The sergeant was the first to recover. He carried down the man he had saved, and saw him sent off to the hospital. . . . Sergeant Vaughan was laid up himself then. He had returned to his work, and finished it, but what he had gone through was too much for human strength. It was spring before he returned to his quarters, to find himself promoted, petted, and made much of.

Everyone joined firefighting efforts—a turn-of-the-century bucket
brigade.

possible to build taller hotels and factories, larger theaters
and other places of entertainment, bigger schools and
hospitals. In short, technology was making it possible to
fit more and more people under a single roof—with all the
implications that had for the dangers of fire.

One of the proudest of these new buildings was the
Iroquois Theater in Chicago. Among the largest and best-
equipped theaters of its day, it opened its doors late in
1903 in time for the holiday crowd. The Christmas show
featured the leading vaudevillian Eddy Foy in a frothy
show called *Mr. Bluebeard.* On December 30, at a Wednesday matinee, Foy looked out on the audience and was
struck by the preponderance of women and children in
the audience—all no doubt enjoying a holiday treat.

The first act had gone well. The audience, a packed
house—more than seventeen hundred seated and at least
two hundred standees in the aisles—were obviously enjoying themselves. Then Foy, offstage for a costume
change, heard a great commotion. As he rushed out of his
dressing room, he heard the terrifying cry of "Fire!" An
arc light twelve or fifteen feet above the stage had blown
a fuse and the sparks had ignited a nearby piece of theat-
rical gauze. The flames, feeding on the 280 oil-painted
gauze backdrops, defied the efforts of stagehands to stop
them.

THE IROQUOIS
THEATER FIRE

CHICAGO
1903

Debris fills the stage of Chicago's
Iroquois Theater after the 1903 fire.

The Iroquois Theater program's boast
was tragically false.

Foy raced onto the stage to calm the audience. He
encouraged the orchestra to go on playing. Burning debris
falling on him soon drove him off, but not before he had
ordered the stagehands to lower the asbestos curtain and
thus separate the burning stage from the audience. As the
curtain came down, however, it caught on a wire, leaving
a twelve-foot gap between it and the floor. By this time
four hundred or so people in the stage company and crew
were trying to get away from the flames. Opening the
backstage doors, including the enormous scenery-loading
door, they created a strong draft that sent a blast of flame
and deadly vapors out through the opening under the
partially lowered asbestos curtain and into the audience.

By this time it was complete pandemonium. The race
for exits was on. There were thirty of them, but many
were virtually useless—either they were unmarked with
lights, or they were obscured by draperies, or they were
locked.

Most of the people on the ground floor were able to
escape even so; but the people in the balcony and gallery
were not as fortunate. Just as in the Brooklyn Theatre fire
more than a quarter of a century earlier, there were too
many people and too few available exits. And just as in
Brooklyn, they trampled one another in their futile rush
to get out.

Within fifteen to twenty minutes all the damage was done. Tragically, 602 people had been killed. Some of them were piled three and four deep in front of exit doors that opened inward. In their rush to get out they had sealed themselves in. Many were jammed into narrow exit halls and staircases where they had been suffocated. Still others had never left their seats, victims of flames that spread so rapidly that they'd never had a chance to move.

Firefighters and other rescue workers carried the bodies out to the sidewalk, laying them side by side. By five o'clock in the afternoon, the lifeless row extended a hundred yards. Catholic priests moved down it administering the last rites to the still unidentified victims.

Of course grief-stricken and angry Chicagoans demanded that an investigation be made into this tragedy, and the findings were quickly translated into a new fire code. No more would Chicago allow doors in public places to open inward—instead they would be equipped with easily operated "panic bars" and open outward. Exits were to be clearly marked and totally unobstructed. Theater personnel were to be drilled in directing people out in quick and orderly fashion. Automatic sprinkler systems were made mandatory. It had taken Chicago twenty-seven years and twice the casualties to learn the Brooklyn Theatre lesson. Luckily, many other cities, both in the United States and all over the world, heeded the lesson of the Iroquois in their theaters—and have thus probably saved thousands of lives.

American technology had also produced what it considered the "fire-resistive" or "fireproof" building. By the turn of the century the people of Baltimore boasted several of these buildings in their business district. It was here that the effectiveness of such fireproofing was put to the test—a test that it failed. On the Sunday morning of February 7, 1904, a small fire was discovered in the basement of one of these fireproof buildings, a drygoods house. Within forty-eight seconds of the alarm, Engine Company No. 15 responded. Taking note of the limited nature of the blaze, firefighters turned a chemical hose on it and looked foreward to being able to get back to their firehouse in good time for lunch.

But there was a terrible surprise in store for them. The burning rubbish on which they were playing the hose contained celluloid novelties, and suddenly they

"FIREPROOF" BUILDINGS' CONFLAGRATION

BALTIMORE
1904

The beginning of the Baltimore conflagration, 1904

burst into flames that shot up the elevator shaft. Seven minutes later these flames set off a powerful explosion on an upper floor, blowing out all the windows in the building as well as shattering all those in the neighborhood. As one contemporary firefighter put it: "It was then seen that the entire house was alight from top to bottom and the flames shooting out through the windows greedily licked the walls of the buildings opposite, which, in their turn, took fire."

A wind growing in force sent the flames across the business district. As flames shot out of the broken windows on the upper stories of one building, they were carried through the broken windows of the next. On and on they traveled. Actually, in many of the affected buildings the lower stories were unscathed while the upper stories were completely gutted.

Bad luck plagued the firefighters. First they lost their leader. Shortly after arriving on the scene their Chief Engineer George W. Horton was felled by an electric jolt from a fallen cable. Then when firefighting companies came pouring in from other communities (as far away as

110

New York), they discovered that their hose couplings did not fit those on the Baltimore hydrants. The visitors were forced either to go down to the harbor and try to draw water from there or to set up some jerry-built reservoir near a hydrant and draw from that. Finally, 152 barrels of whiskey caught fire and the burning spirits flooded into the street, destroying three pieces of apparatus.

The fire raged on, consuming block after block, through Sunday night and far into Monday. Tugs raced through the harbor trying to move boats anchored there from danger. Other boats steaming toward the harbor and seeing the city in flames quickly turned back to sea to avoid being consumed themselves.

Late Monday afternoon thirty-six fire companies and a fireboat made a final desperate stand at Jones Falls, "a little dirty, bad-smelling stream, which had never served a useful purpose." There the firefighters were finally able to stop the onrush of flames, some thirty hours after they had burst to life.

The fire had covered approximately 140 acres, burning out eighty city blocks. Miraculously no firefighters had been killed, although forty were injured. Losses were estimated at $100 million (nearly $650 million today). And the faith of Baltimore's people in their "fireproof" buildings had been thoroughly shaken. But nothing could have withstood the estimated 2,200° to 2,800° heat that the fire had produced or the invasion of the buildings by fire from the outside.

Several more major-city fires occurred all over the country in the next few years—in Chelsea, Massachusetts, in Paris, Texas, in Atlanta, Georgia, in Astoria, Oregon, and in Nome, Alaska. But better construction materials, upgraded fire laws and zoning, and improved firefighting techniques and equipment would limit their number and extent. From now on, major American fires would, with some important exceptions, be confined to smaller, often enclosed areas. These fires would often be less costly in money but just as often much more costly in lives.

One such fire involved the burning of the *General Slocum*, an excursion steamer that regularly plied its way up the East River in New York, taking groups to picnic in the countryside. Made entirely of wood, she was a paddle wheeler 250 feet long and 70 feet wide.

Fireboat pumps stream of water into smoking wreck of the *General Slocum*, New York, 1904.

THE GENERAL SLOCUM FIRE

NEW YORK
1904

On the morning of June 15, 1904, she stood gleaming in the sun, waiting at a recreation pier to take on this day's merrymakers—a Sunday school group from St. Mark's German Lutheran Church. A German band played a sprightly polka as the gay crowds began boarding. It was a Wednesday, so the picnickers were mainly women and children—the 50 men on board were vastly outnumbered by the roughly 565 women and 745 children.

When everyone was on board, Captain William Van Schaick directed his boat away from the pier and toward the picnic grounds. The women settled down to chat and to get their abundant supplies of food in readiness. Children raced along the length and breadth of the ship, up and down from one deck to another. The ship's crew of twenty-seven went about their work. People on shore watched the happy scene and waved at the ship as it passed them.

But observers' friendly smiles quickly changed to looks of horror. Puffs of smoke were coming out of the ship's bow and no one on board seemed aware of it. Other boats frantically tooted their whistles, but the *General Slocum* sailed blithely on.

Finally some little boys noticed the smoke coming out of a cabin on the main deck and raced aft to find a member of the crew to tell. The crewmember opened the door to the cabin—in which lamps, rope, and oil were stored—and the oxygen that raced in flashed the fire. Two crewmen now raced for fire hoses to train on the blaze. But when they finally succeeded in getting water to run through the hose, its rotted fibers crumbled in their hands, and no water reached the flames.

By this time people on shore had sent in the alarm. The nearest fire company came thundering out of their firehouse and galloped to the end of a close-by pier. The *Zophar Mills,* a powerful fireboat, came churning up the river in hot pursuit of the burning paddle wheeler. Other boats in the area also gave chase, to lend what assistance they could. Everyone expected Captain Van Schaick to steer his boat toward shore, where help could be given. Instead, they watched in disbelief as he continued on his midstream course upriver. The firefighters on the pier stared after the burning boat in total helplessness and frustration.

On board the scene was even worse than the firefighters could imagine. As the boat continued plowing into the wind, the flames spread ever backward. People desperately crowded toward the stern, where many were forced overboard, frequently into the path of the churning paddle wheels. Then the superstructure on which many of them were standing collapsed and sent them into the raging fire below.

A few men on board who were keeping their heads went for the life preservers. Like the hoses, these were old and totally useless, and they crumbled to bits as the now panic-stricken passengers grabbed for them. Another man was tossing children to the waiting arms of the crewmen on boats that were trying to catch up with the blazing paddle wheeler. Mothers were throwing their children overboard and jumping in after them.

Rescue workers carry bodies ashore after the burning of the *General Slocum.*

After what must have seemed an eternity, Captain Van Schaick beached the boat on North Brother Island, a medical station for patients with contagious diseases. Nurses and doctors waded or swam out to try to rescue victims. The firefighters who had been left back on the pier had sailed after the burning steamer in any boats they could commandeer. Now catching up with it, they also went to the rescue. So did the *Zophar Mills.*

The rescuers dragged body after body up on shore—some living, many dead. Other bodies were still trapped in the burning hulk or in the paddle wheels and boxes. All of the crew but one escaped death. But a staggering number of the passengers did not—more than one thousand of the nearly fourteen hundred who had so gaily set out that morning were or soon would be dead.

The investigation that followed told a disgusting story of incompetence, misjudgment, and greed. The crew had been inexperienced and unprepared. Captain Van Schaick was later convicted for neglecting to train them in proper fire drill (though he was not convicted of two counts of manslaughter stemming from his failure to get his boat to shore sooner). The ship, supposedly inspected only a month before, was later found to have been "made entirely of wood, built in 1891 [without] fireproof hatches or bulkheads. All upperworks were of light wood, painted over many times and highly flammable. The hose was several years old and of the cheapest grade; the fire buckets on the main deck were not only out of reach, they had no water in them. The mate was not a licensed officer." Obviously, other major villains in the tragedy were the inspectors who had somehow allowed the *General Slocum* to pass fire inspection (whatever fines they had levied for violations of the steamer had been magically reduced from $1500 to $25). The guilty inspectors were dismissed, and future ship inspection was made more demanding, but once again an unbearable price had been paid to provide the fire protection the public so greatly needed.

EARTHQUAKE AND FIRE

SAN FRANCISCO
1906

The *General Slocum* tragedy could be blamed in large part on the acts of men, but the awesome devastation of San Francisco in 1906 was triggered by what insurance parlance calls an act of God.

Shortly after five o'clock on the morning of April 18, San Franciscans were jolted into the most terrifying experience of their lives. One woman described what happened to her:

> I was awakened out of peaceful sleep into a paralysis of fear by the violent and continued rocking of bed, of floors, of walls, of furniture, by the sounds of crashing chimneys, falling ornaments and pictures, breaking glass and the startled screams of women and children. As if with a sudden impact, I felt my bed struck from the north and then heave violently. I jumped out, putting my hands out to steady myself, but the opposite walls seemed to move away from me. The floor rocked like a boat on a choppy sea, the violence of the motion increased and seemed ever and again to take a fresh start. It seems as if it would never end—and yet it lasted but two minutes.

A man who was walking down a San Francisco street with some friends described the scene outdoors:

> Of a sudden we found ourselves staggering and reeling. It was as if the earth was slipping gently from under our feet. Then came a sickening swaying of the earth that threw us flat upon our faces. . . . We could not get on our feet. I looked in dazed fashion around me. I saw for an instant the big buildings in what looked like a crazy dance. Then it seemed as though my head were split with the roar that crashed into my ears. Big buildings were crumbling as one might crush a biscuit in one's hand.

The San Andreas fault, the fissure that runs the length of California, was shifting under San Francisco. Within seconds its action sent buildings crashing down, buckled streets, ruptured gas pipes and water mains, ripped down lines, thus sending live wires flying—all of

Collapsed buildings and smoke from fires confront San Franciscoans after the 1906 earthquake.

San Francisco's hilly streets are lined with rubble after earthquake and fire devastated the city.

which combined to set fires all over the city. In those seconds it also knocked out nearly every fire alarm in the city.

San Francisco's firefighters were out, six hundred strong, immediately, but with hundreds of fires to fight and the water mains useless, their efforts were almost in vain. Still they worked on, doing all they could, including rescuing hundreds of people trapped in the rubble. Firefighters were also able to save the wharf area using water from the harbor.

Soon the many separate fires in the downtown area combined into a three-mile front that moved relentlessly across the stricken city. The mansions of San Francisco's rich and the wooden shacks of its poor fell before it. Soon the U.S. Army moved in to protect property from looting and to create fire breaks with dynamite and shelling.

As had happened in so many fires before, these breaks were not successful. Shattered buildings merely provided better kindling than whole ones. And so the fire burned on through Wednesday and into Thursday.

It was then that the San Francisco firefighters, assembled with fire companies from several California communities, were able to make a major stand against the flames. Just as at Jones Falls in Baltimore two years before, if they could not hold here, the fire would consume the entire city. By this time some of the ruptured water mains had been repaired, and broad Van Ness Avenue was broadened still more to five hundred feet through the use of bombardment. For ten hours the firefighting force held fast against the fire until finally they won control.

All through Friday they continued to fight fires, sometimes passing out from sheer exhaustion but rising to fight again. Finally on Saturday morning, after three full days of fire, a rain drenched the city, and San Francisco could turn to the job of rebuilding (once again challenging the San Andreas fault).

The scope of the rebuilding job was overpowering. Nearly five square miles of the city, three thousand acres, were destroyed, at a loss estimated at $350 million (nearly $2.3 billion today). Over the 520-city-block area, twenty-five thousand buildings, half of them residences, were in ruins. About three hundred thousand San Franciscans roamed the streets homeless or left the city entirely.

Nearly five hundred people were killed in that bitter, brief time. Many perished beneath crumbling walls, but most were consumed by the pervasive fires. Many others were caught looting and shot on the spot.

LAKE VIEW ELEMENTARY SCHOOL

COLLINWOOD, OHIO
1908

By the early 1900s the one-room schoolhouse had long since given way to multi-room, multi-level structures in much of the United States—and many of these newer schools were built with little or no regard for fire hazards. One of them was the Lake View Elementary School in the Ohio community of Collinwood, population eight thousand. The enrollment of 325 pupils had outgrown the school's two stories of classrooms, so the

IMPORTANT FIRES IN THE UNITED STATES SINCE 1906

Collinwood, Ohio, schoolhouse fire, 1908 (178 killed, most of them children)

Chicago Stockyards fire, 1910 (21 firefighters killed)

Triangle Shirtwaist Factory, 1911 (146 killed)

Black Tom Pier fire, 1916 (suspected World War I sabotage)

Minnesota forest fires, 1918 (559 killed)

Wall Street explosion, 1920 (40 killed; "Red Scare")

Cleveland Clinic fire, 1929 (125 killed by fumes from burning X-rays)

Columbus, Ohio, prison fire, 1930 (320 convicts killed)

S.S. *Morro Castle* fire at sea, 1934 (134 killed)

Cocoanut Grove (Boston) nightclub fire, 1942 (492 killed)

Hartford Circus fire, 1944 (163 killed)

La Salle Hotel (Chicago) fire, 1946 (61 killed)

Hotel Winecoff (Atlanta) fire, 1946 (119 killed)

Texas City, Texas, 1947 (468 killed, including entire vol. F.D.)

St. Anthony's Hospital (Illinois) fire, 1949 (77 killed)

Our Lady of the Angels (Chicago) school fire, 1958 (93 killed, most of them children)

23rd Street fire, New York, 1966 (12 firefighters killed)

Riots, from 1965 to 1968 (fire as protest)

Philadelphia storage tank fire, 1975 (8 firefighters killed)

Kentucky nightclub fire, 1977, (165 killed)

attic was also pressed into service. For these students and their nine teachers, only three exits were available, a front and a rear door, both of which opened inward, and one uncovered fire escape which came down from the third floor.

At nine thirty in the morning of March 4, 1908, students and teachers were settled down to their day's work when the fire bell sounded. Accustomed to fire drills, the students lined up and followed their teachers' instructions to move out into the narrow halls.

There to their surprise they were greeted with heavy black smoke and with the terrible realization that this was not a drill but the real thing. A fire that had started in the basement had made rapid progress through the brick structure, and within moments it had cut off exit through the front door with a wall of flame. On seeing this the students panicked. In their race for the rear door they trampled one another. Those who finally fought their

way to the door found it locked, and their schoolmates charging up behind them crushed them against the sealed exit.

Teachers tried to regain order, but it was a losing battle. One who was directing her class down the second-floor hall saw that the flames racing up the stairs toward them made passage down impossible. Quickly she redirected her charges up to the third floor where she handed them out onto the fire escape and safety.

But other students were not so lucky. As horrified parents rushed toward the blazing schoolbuilding, they saw their children at the windows, trapped and pleading to be saved. Women rushed for ladders. Men sought to break in the doors held fast by the bodies of the children piled up against them. Parent after parent had to watch as his or her child seemed close to safety and then fell back into the flames.

After too long a delay the volunteer fire department of Collinwood arrived. As they drew up a sickening crash was heard—the interior of the school had just collapsed,

The Lake View Elementary School is filled with smoke as Collinwood, Ohio, firefighters train hoses on the fire, 1908.

119

sending children on the upper floors tumbling into the inferno that was the basement and first floor.

The fire burned on for three hours, but it had already taken its terrible toll. Only eighty children had escaped injury. About seventy had burns and other injuries from which they would eventually recover. That left the staggering total of 175 six- to fourteen-year-olds dead in the ruins of Lake View.

The news of this carnage, of families losing one, two, and even three children, frightened other Americans into examining the fire protection offered by their own schools. As a result new fire laws were drawn up and new standards for school construction were set up in communities all over the country. This new concern for school safety unfortunately did not end all loss of life in school fires, but it surely saved untold lives over the years.

LEATHER FACTORY FIRE

PHILADELPHIA
1910

No one would deny that a fire statistic of 175 children killed is an appalling one, but perhaps there is another one that is even worse—the year-in, year-out statistic of American firefighters killed in the line of duty, about three hundred sixty-five annually, or one every day of the year. One of the greatest single numbers of firefighters lost occurred in a twenty-four-hour period in 1910. In two fires, one in Philadelphia and one in Chicago, a total of thirty-five firefighters were killed.

On December 21 a fire in a leather factory in Philadelphia burned to such a heat that it crumbled the mortar in the brick walls and sent them crashing in on the

New Orleans firefighters make efficient use of a fire cistern during a furniture store blaze in 1908.

Ice-covered engine and firefighters battle both cold and flames at the Equitable Building in New York, January 1912.

firefighters battling the blaze. Their comrades succeeded in digging a few of them out alive, one after being buried for twelve hours. But sadly, after many hours of frantic digging, the bodies of the dead firefighters began to mount, until there were fourteen lying on the rubble-covered street in front of the factory.

The following night in Chicago, a watchman discovered a fire in a cold storage plant in that city's sprawling stockyards. After hearing an explosion he turned in the alarm and fled. Within minutes the firefighters who had arrived on the scene knew that they faced a big one and a 4-11 (a 4th alarm) was struck. As the early hours of the morning dragged by, more and more companies were called—at least forty in all.

Chicago's Fire Marshal James Horan had taken command, and with his Second Assistant William J. Burroughs he led his men to fight the flames from under a heavy wooden canopy. As the men crowded in there, a firefighter atop the canopy saw the walls of the warehouse bulge. Shouting a warning to the others, he jumped. But it was too late for them. The cold air in the warehouse had expanded with the heat, creating an explosion that sent a wall of white-hot bricks crashing down on Horan and his men, killing them instantly. Another fifty men were also buried in the debris, and their voices could be heard calling for rescue.

Soon the adjoining buildings were aflame too, so the firefighters had two battles on their hands—one to quench the blaze and one to save their buried comrades. For sixteen hours the fire burned on as a railroad wrecking

STOCKYARDS FIRE

CHICAGO
1910

THE TRIANGLE FIRE

NEW YORK
1911

Left: Hose towers vainly shoot water toward the upper floors of the Asch building, where 146 clothing workers died, New York, 1911.

train and several steam shovels dug through the smoldering ruins.

When the fire was finally extinguished, Horan's firefighters could turn all of their efforts to the search for their leader and the other missing men. More than fifty of these searchers dropped from exhaustion and had to be carried away from the intense heat. But one by one the badly mutilated bodies were found—twenty-one of them —and frantic relatives were told of their loved ones' fate. The last body found was that of Captain Dennis N. Doyle. His son, Pipeman Edward Doyle, collapsed when he was told the news. Young Doyle had not left the fire scene for thirty-six hours, all the while searching not only for his father but also for his brother. The falling walls had also killed Pipeman Nicholas Doyle.

Chicago was still mourning its loss when news of another fire tragedy shocked and saddened the American people. It happened in New York City on March 25, 1911, and this time the victims were mostly young girls and women aged thirteen to twenty.

Right: A twisted and useless fire escape after the Triangle fire.

Police cover bodies of women who had jumped from the flaming eighth floor.

The Asch Building was a ten-story structure that stood near the city's famous Washington Square. Designed originally as a place where mercantile goods were to be sold and stored, it now housed several "loft factories," the largest of which was the Triangle Shirtwaist Company occupying the top three floors.

On this particular Saturday afternoon, the rest of the building was empty, since the other tenants worked a five-and-a-half-day week. But the Triangle owners demanded a full six-day week of their mostly immigrant workers, so over six hundred employees still labored over their crowded work tables, cutting and sewing flimsy materials into the fashionable ladies' blouses of the day. At 4:45, just as the workers were getting ready to leave, someone spotted a fire smoldering in a rag bin on the eighth floor. A few of them grabbed fire buckets and tried to put it out, but the flames had already leapt to the tissue paper and cloth scraps that covered the wooden work tables and wooden floors.

Within moments the eighth floor was ablaze, and the young cutters and sewers were racing for the only two doorways off the floor. One opened into a passageway purposely kept narrow so that the girls could pass through it only one at a time—a measure designed by the owners so that everyone's handbag could be checked each night for any stolen goods. This led to two small elevators, each capable of holding only about a dozen people, and to a narrow set of winding stairs guarded by a door that opened inward. The other doorway also led to a staircase, but as the now panic-stricken workers tried to open that door, they found it bolted shut from the outside —another management measure, this time to guard against any employees sneaking out for a break.

Even against these terrible odds, most of the eighth floor workers were able to escape with their lives. On the ninth floor, though, it was a different story. There flames licking up from below entered the windows, setting fire to the patterns and blouses that hung there. In no time that floor was almost completely ablaze, and the nearly three hundred workers there had even less time to escape than their co-workers downstairs. Everywhere their attempts to flee were thwarted. They too faced the locked door and the narrow passageway, but by this time the narrow stairway was full of smoke and the elevators were already too full to take on more passengers.

In the face of the advancing flames the screaming young women did desperate things. More than thirty of them jumped into the elevator shaft, crushing themselves and others and putting the elevators they sought to ride down, out of commission. Some tried to use the building's single fire escape, but the intense heat had softened it to the point that it twisted itself away from the wall, sending the would be escapees tumbling into the courtyard below. Another sixty climbed out on window ledges where they hovered until the flames caught them. Then, to the horror of the crowd below, they stepped off the ledges and came crashing down nine stories to the pavement. Firefighters, on the scene within three minutes, valiantly tried to catch them in life nets, but the hundred-foot drop was just too great. (It was calculated that the bodies of three of these young girls, falling from that height, landed with a dead weight of sixteen tons.)

Firefighters could do little to battle the fire from the ground—their aerial ladders went only as high as the sixth floor and their water towers to the seventh—but they raced up the stairs with their hose in a mad dash to douse the flames in time to save more people from jumping. Within eighteen minutes they had the fire under control, but it was too late. Nearly 150 Triangle employees were dead or dying and another 70 were seriously injured.

Once again greed and human insensitivity had taken an incredible toll of 146 lives. In the investigation that inevitably followed, it was discovered that no sprinkler system had been installed in the building because it would have cost five thousand dollars. A third staircase was not constructed, as required by law, because the architect argued that the single fire escape fulfilled this requirement. And of course the locking of doors was done to save a few dollars in pilfering and a few stolen minutes of rest for the dollar-per-day employees.

But once again tragedy led to change. Within a short time after the disaster thirty new ordinances were incorporated into New York's fire code, and many other communities followed suit.

Spectators at the Triangle fire probably were too horrified to take much note of the equipment brought to fight it, but two of the pieces there were a sign that one age of firefighting was ending and another was beginning. Two of the engines fighting the flames were motorized rather than horse-drawn.

The conversion from horses and steam to gas-powered pumpers in the early 1900s had certain parallels with the conversion from hand pumpers to steam in the mid-1800s. Both changeovers were vehemently opposed by firefighters at first—on both mechanical and sentimental grounds. Just as the earlier firefighters had trusted their own pumping over that of steam, so later firefighters trusted their well-trained fire horses over the new internal combustion engines that broke down with some regu-

Early motorized fire engine, an Ahrens Fox

Demonstration of an early tower aerial ladder, 1920s

Fireboats, 1920s

larity. Then too, how could they ever love a smelly motor the way they loved their well-matched teams—Spike and Caesar and Blue Bob?

But just as the first changeover was inevitable, so was the second. As the motorized equipment improved, it supplanted the horses. One by one, firehouses across the country bade sad farewells to the horses they had trained and loved, and then reluctantly accepted their new and gleaming gasoline pumpers and motorized hook and ladder trucks. By the 1920s the last of the fire horses were gone—sold off to pull junk wagons or delivery carts. Occasionally one of them would be seen racing through the streets, a milk wagon clattering behind him, as he went to answer the clanging of a fire gong.

During this age of transition one of the most destructive fires to take place in the United States was not the result of accident or greed or stupidity—its cause was sabotage.

In 1916 Americans were still tenaciously hanging on to their neutrality as the First World War raged in Europe. However, they were willing to stretch being neutral to the point that they were producing great quantities of munitions for the Allied countries. Many of these munitions were shipped by rail to the port of New York, where they were stored briefly and then loaded onto barges, from which they were loaded onto transatlantic ships. In the early hours of Sunday, July 30, 1916, thirty-two freight cars and ten barges filled with two million pounds of explosives were stored on Black Tom, a peninsula jutting out from the New Jersey shore a quarter mile from the Statue of Liberty and a half mile from Ellis Island.

At about 12:40 A.M., a watchman there spotted a fire, and within a very short time the Jersey City Fire Department responded to his alarm. A puzzling fire awaited them; it persisted in spite of their efforts to stop its march toward the munitions cars and barges. Before long it reached some explosives, and soon the firefighters were dodging shells and shrapnel as they battled on. Tugboats tried to tow the barges to safety, but the tug men too were dodging shells.

BLACK TOM PIER FIRE

NEW JERSEY
1916

Fireboats soak schooner during Black Tom pier fire, New Jersey, 1916.

Hulk burns offshore after Black Tom explosion.

At 2:08 the inevitable happened. A thunderous explosion rocked the area, flattening the firefighters and destroying thirteen warehouses, several freight cars and barges, several pieces of firefighting equipment, and Black Tom's one and only water main. Glass was shattered in buildings more than six miles away, and both the Statue of Liberty and Ellis Island were bombarded by a barrage of shells.

Still, the firefighters worked on, knowing that at any moment another explosion might occur, taking them with it. At 2:40 it came, but once again they were miraculously spared to fight on.

By this time, explosive-filled barges had burned away from the pier and were drifting into the path of other craft in the harbor. Fireboats followed after to intercept them before they could do any more damage. Once the fireboats had succeeded, they approached the Black Tom shore to train their heavy streams on the still raging fire, one of them taking a shell in the pilot house as they did.

The fire burned on for two weeks, killing six people and doing $20 million (nearly $106 million today) in damage. As time passed, painstaking detective work proved that the Black Tom disaster had been the work of a ring of German saboteurs, one of them Franz von Papen, a man who one day would be instrumental in bringing Adolf Hitler to power.

Firefighters train streams of water on rubble after Black Tom explosion.

Two years after the Black Tom holocaust, the worst American fire of the twentieth century, in terms of loss of life, ravaged the forests of Northern Minnesota. In many ways this fire was virtually a carbon copy of the inferno that had wiped out vast areas of the Wisconsin woodlands around Peshtigo forty-seven years earlier. The causes of the two were the same—exceptional dryness, smaller fires burning freely in the forest, and a freshening breeze that spread the flames, feeding upon their growing heat until the breeze became a sixty-mile-an-hour firestorm.

The Minnesota fires burnt out about the same amount of land that the Peshtigo fire had—approximately fifteen hundred square miles. As in the 1871 conflagration, several towns were totally burned out and numerous farms destroyed.

Thanks to trains and motorcars, not available to the victims of Peshtigo, many more people were able to flee the raging forest fires to safety. Even so, a total of 559 people, half of the Peshtigo toll, were killed.

Throughout American history, firefighters have been called into disasters brought on by a variety of causes other than the accidental starting of a fire—from the time of the malcontent firebugs of the Colonial period to the draft rioters of the Civil War to the Black Tom saboteurs of World War I. During and after that war, American

FOREST FIRES

MINNESOTA
1918

WALL STREET EXPLOSION

NEW YORK
1920

Anarchist's bomb intended for J. P. Morgan brought death and destruction to Wall Street, New York, 1920.

firefighters were pressed into service by the work of yet another group—the political terrorists who gave the United States the era of the "Red Scare."

Wall Street, the financial capital of the nation, had long been a target for the many amorphous radical groups that had frightened Americans for years—the anarchists, communists, and socialists. On September 16, 1920, as the clock on the steeple of the Wall Street area's famous Trinity Church was about to strike noon, a driver pulled his canvas-covered, horse-drawn cart up opposite the House of Morgan, the symbol of the power of money. Throwing the reins over the back of the horse, the driver leaped out of the cart and disappeared into the lunchtime crowd.

In a few minutes, just as the last toll from the church steeple had rung, a tremendous explosion shattered the calm. As it reverberated, a great ball of fire leapt skyward. Shrapnel tore through the crowd and into the surrounding buildings with a force so great that one piece went

BATTALION CHIEF MICHAEL J. CORRIGAN
CHICAGO FIRE DEPARTMENT

Another incident related to the "Red Scare" took place in the Auditorium Theater in Chicago in 1917. Battalion Chief Michael J. Corrigan was standing at the back of the packed house where he saw a flash and a flame leap up among the seats near the main aisle about twenty feet from him.

"Keep your seats," he shouted to the audience, perhaps remembering the scene at the Iroquois Theater fourteen years earlier. Then, racing to the fire site, he discovered that there was a bomb under one of the seats, its fuse still burning, and that several people were trying unsuccessfully to kick it out into the aisle.

Coolly and bravely, Corrigan got down on his hands and knees and reached under the seat, pulling the bomb out carefully. He extinguished the burning wick. Throwing his coat over it, he carried it out as a tense audience followed his every step.

As soon as Corrigan had defused the potential killer, a grateful theater manager begged him to return to the theater and go onstage to explain that now all was well. By doing so, he "averted what might have been a serious calamity," in the words of the commendation the department presented him.

through a thirty-fourth-floor window. Thousands of panes of glass splintered and showered down on the pavement.

As the quaking subsided, those people who could picked themselves up from their plaster-strewn office floors or from the glass-and-stone-littered ground. Thirty others would never pick themselves up again. Of one man who had passed close to the cart, only one finger and a ring remained. Another man, sitting in an office window, had been decapitated. Of the horse only a pool of blood and his horseshoes could be found.

Within six minutes the fire department was on the scene. There was little fire to fight, but there was a great deal of rescue work to be done. Everywhere people were tangled in the masses of debris that had fallen.

The investigation that followed turned up very little other than the cause of the blast and its devastation. The cart had contained a TNT bomb powerful enough to send five hundred pounds of metal pieces flying in all directions for a distance of as much as half a mile. The driver was never found nor was any evidence to tie a particular group to the outrage. But the assumption that it was

Refugees from fire, Boise, Idaho, 1920s

planned and executed by radicals alienated Americans even further from radical causes.

Unlike the cart driver on Wall Street, whose ambition was to maim and kill, Dr. George W. Crile chose as his life's work to cure and save. During World War I he had gone off to France to work in a military hospital, treating fighting men who were the victims of war's old weapons—gunshot, shrapnel, bayonet—and of a new one —poisonous gas. On returning to Ohio after the war, Crile joined with three other doctors to establish the Cleveland Clinic. There he hoped to provide patients with renewed life and health.

By 1929 the medical establishment occupied not only the four-story Clinic building, but also a separate hospital. On the morning of May 15 of that year, a steam fitter with the unlikely name of Bufferty Boggs was summoned to the Clinic building to fix a steam leak in a basement room where X-ray plates were stored. Unable to locate a leak, Boggs left, only to be called back a few hours later to look again. When he arrived back in the storage room, he and a Clinic employee heard a "sputtering hiss" and looked up toward the ceiling. Later Boggs described what happened:

> We saw a big patch of yellow stuff, probably four or five feet in diameter. It was sticky-looking, and puffs of yellow smoke shot out of it at intervals, going downward, then up, as tho it was lighter than air. I noticed then that the ceiling was dripping. We saw no flames then. . . .

CLEVELAND CLINIC FIRE

CLEVELAND
1929

Rescue workers carry patients from the Cleveland Clinic, 1929.

The "sticky puffs of yellow smoke" that the two men spotted were coming from the stored X-ray plates. Made of highly inflammable nitrate celluloid film, the plates had somehow begun to smolder, and as they did, they gave off nitrogen dioxide, the most insidious irritant gas known at the time. Even as the two men stood there, the noxious fumes were spreading through air vents into the Clinic's rooms and quietly felling unsuspecting patients and medical personnel.

Within moments two explosions, one right after the other, ripped through the storage room, sending great balls of smoke upward into the Clinic. When the explosions sounded, Dr. Crile had just completed an operation. Running from the hospital, still clad in his surgical gown and cap, he saw great yellow clouds billowing out of the Clinic. With crushing certainty his war experience told him what they contained—poison gas.

A three-alarm fire signal brought much of Cleveland's firefighting force to the scene immediately. The fumes barred the firefighters from entering the building, but, risking the noxious clouds that threatened them, they raised ladders and spread life nets for the terrified people clustered at the Clinic windows.

133

A *Cleveland News* reporter described what was happening to those those still inside:*

> They were trapt.
>
> Men and women rushed for the elevator and stairways. But before they reached either, the majority of them toppled over, unconscious from the effects of the fumes.
>
> Others dashed for windows in the hope of getting a breath of air that would drive out the poison from their lungs. But in most instances they were too weak to raise or break the windows when they reached them.
>
> People in the street, attracted by the explosion and clouds of yellow smoke pouring from the building, saw many of the victims beat weakly against the glass panes of the windows and then drop back to the floors—dead or dying.
>
> One woman crawled to the ledge of a window and attempted to jump to a waiting fire net, but a wave of yellow gas enveloped her and she toppled inward.
>
> The stairways leading to fresh air and safety were piled high with struggling, gasping men and women—their desperate efforts to move onward and outward failing as gas inhalations choked them.
>
> More than thirty victims were piled in a heap in front of the elevator shaft on the third floor. Their frantic sounding of the elevator signal had brought no response. The operator was dying.
>
> Women too weak to walk dropt to their hands and knees and crawled along the marble corridors in a futile struggle to drag their poison-saturated bodies to safety.
>
> Unlike most disasters where human beings are trapt by fire, there were few screams of anguish and suffering inside the chamber of death. It was because of the gas. Within a few seconds after inhalation, the fumes had stifled ability to cry out. A fit of coughing—then unconsciousness and death.

The death toll at the Cleveland Clinic was 125, most of them asphyxiated by the poisonous gas rather than killed by the fire that followed the explosions. A new medical breakthrough—the X-ray—had worked to take life rather than save it.

Nitrate celluloid was never used for X-ray film again —a harmless acetate film could be substituted for it—but firefighters had learned that they now had a new enemy, as insidious as fire or smoke. The chemical compounds that science was developing in the name of progress could be killers when they came into contact with fire.

Within a year and within 125 miles of the Cleveland Clinic tragedy, fire visited another disaster on the state of Ohio. Right in the midst of its capital city of Columbus stood the Ohio State Penitentiary, where, in the tough depression year of 1930, well over four thousand men

OHIO STATE PENITENTIARY

COLUMBUS
1930

*This excerpt, by Don K. Rennels, is from *Cleveland News,* May 16 or 17, 1929

FIREFIGHTERS' COURAGE

AT THE CLEVELAND CLINIC

Among the first firefighters on the scene that terrible day in Cleveland were Battalion Chief Michael Graham and his men. Not knowing what they faced inside the Clinic, Graham ordered one of his men to put on a gas mask and go into the building to find out. In less than a minute the man staggered out, coughing and choking.

"Can't make it, it's killing," he shuddered, and fell into the Chief's arms.

With this Chief Graham knew that trying to get in any of the entrances was hopeless. They would have to find a different way.

"Up the ladders, up the ladders! Get them from the top," Graham shouted.

Braving the noxious clouds that swirled around him, firefighter Louis Hildebrand raced up a motorized ladder to the roof. There he ran to the skylight and looked down.

"I never hope to have to look at anything so horrifying again," he said. "Lord help me, as far down the stairway as you could see were bodies, bodies, bodies. Twisted arms and legs, screaming men and women. . . . Bodies and screams."

Thirty or so patients, rushing toward the roof to escape the fumes that rolled upward after them, had jammed themselves so closely together that they could not move.

Soon Hildebrand was joined on the roof by firefighters Howard McAllister and Peter Rogers, who hacked their way through the skylight and lowered themselves by ropes into the mass of suffering humanity. Chief Graham was lowered in after them.

"It took three firemen to force a way down that stairway and to lift the top one to men on the roof," Chief Graham related. "For five minutes we were lifting those bodies to the skylight before we could get to the third floor, where the screaming was the worst."

On reaching the third floor, Graham ordered pulmotors to be brought in to revive the victims where they lay. As one group of firefighters stood alongside, training their hose on the flames to beat them back, another group battled to get air into the lungs of the stricken before it was too late.

The fast and courageous action of Cleveland's firefighters that day saved at least as many victims as were lost and probably many more.

Ladders compete for space on hospital building as patient is lifted through window.

were held prisoner—nearly three times the fifteen hundred for which the bleak fortress was designed. In an attempt to alleviate this dangerous and unhealthy overcrowding, the state had decided to add an extension to the six-story cell block. Wooden scaffolding ran up the prison wall, and work had begun in earnest.

At about 5:20 in the evening of April 21, one of the convicts told the guards that a fire had begun in the scaffolding. Unfortunately, this particular man was known as "a great kidder," so the guards laughingly chose to ignore his alarm. But as time passed and the timbers blazed on, the cry of "Wolf" was finally heeded, and at six o'clock, the warden's daughter turned in the fire alarm.

At this point the last of the prisoners were just returning from their dinner, to be locked into their cells by six o'clock in accordance with a firm prison rule. But as they learned of the fire that threatened them, they fought with the guards to be left free to flee if necessary. Prisoners already locked in shouted to be let out. Guards—torn between their fear of allowing prisoners to escape and their uncertainty over the seriousness of the fire—did not know what to do. They had never been trained for the possibility of a fire in the prison. To add to the problem, the guard who had the key that would open all the locks adamantly refused to let it be used.

Outside the cell block a strong wind sent flames racing from the scaffolding across the tar-papered wooden

A prison guard refused to open the cells at the Ohio State Penitentiary, where 320 prisoners died in 1930.

roof of the supposedly "fireproof" prison. Smoke and flames ate their way down into the upper tier, engulfing prisoners trapped in their locked cells. Their screams of agony resounded through the prison. First they begged to be saved. Then, as flames made getting to them impossible, they pleaded to be shot before the fire reached them. Two of them, preferring suicide to the flames, cut their own throats with contraband knives.

The guards, at last convinced of the need to free the prisoners, ran down the corridors, unlocking what cells they could. (The locks in some had become so hot that they had warped, and the keys could not open them. The trapped prisoners were left to their fate.) The guards then marched the convicts out into the now crowded courtyard.

Within two minutes of receiving the alarm, Columbus's firefighters were on the scene, trying to get into the cell block to free more prisoners and to extinguish the blaze. But prisoners in the courtyard, maddened by their close call with death, turned on them, attacking the men who had come to help and cutting the hose line that could save their fellow prisoners. The firefighters endured further delay while the guards used tear gas and clubs to regain control over the mob.

It was two hours before the firefighters were able to bring the fire under control. During that time they had not only fought the flames, but they had also used acetylene torches to free the locks that trapped still more prisoners behind bars. And they had begun the terrible job of recovering the bodies of men who had truly been given the death penalty—320 of them, the victims of overcrowded conditions and unprepared guards.

It is probable the Ohio State Penitentiary guards had not been trained to deal with fire because of the mistaken idea that the prison was fireproof. However, the crew of the S.S. *Morro Castle*, a cruise ship plying its way between Havana and New York, were not trained to deal with fire for another, though equally ill-considered, reason: Captain Robert R. Wilmott did not want to disturb his pleasure-seeking passengers. In his view, fire drills and boat drills only excited passengers, and "excitement brings panic." Besides, such drills were unnecessary on his ship because, according to him, "You're safer here than crossing Times Square or South Street."

S.S. MORRO CASTLE

NEW JERSEY
1934

Lifeboat and Coast Guard dory loaded with survivors of the *Morro Castle* row away from the burning ship.

On September 8, 1934, the people aboard the *Morro Castle*—318 passengers and 240 crew members—would come to see Wilmott's mindless optimism for what it was.

Two days earlier the *Morro Castle* had sailed out of Havana harbor on the second and final leg of its Labor Day cruise. Many of the passengers had brought with them gallon jugs of fine Cuban rum, available so cheaply on the island. Many of the crew members had with them supplies of dope, also readily available there. Indeed, it was rumored that some of the crew even paid to work the *Morro Castle* so that they could smuggle the highly profitable dope into the lucrative New York market.

On Friday evening, September 7, as the passengers were preparing for the gala parties that would celebrate their final night out, they learned that Captain Wilmott had died suddenly and therefore the parties were being canceled. With spirits undampened by the captain's death, however, many people decided to hold their own parties, where they consumed prodigious quantities of rum. By the early hours of Saturday morning, countless passengers had staggered off to their cabins to sleep off the effects of their partying so that they could manage to disembark later that day in New York. Outside, sheets of rain, driven by a twenty-knot wind, washed down the ship.

Then, at about 2:30 A.M., a fire was discovered in the ship's writing room. (There is evidence today that it was started deliberately by a crew member.) From that point on the flames spread quickly, a result of the crew's ineptitude and the newly dead captain's disdain for fire precau-

Left: Spectators fill the Asbury Park beach to watch the liner burn, 1934.

Below: Firefighters pump streams of water into the still-burning *Morro Castle* five days after the fire had started.

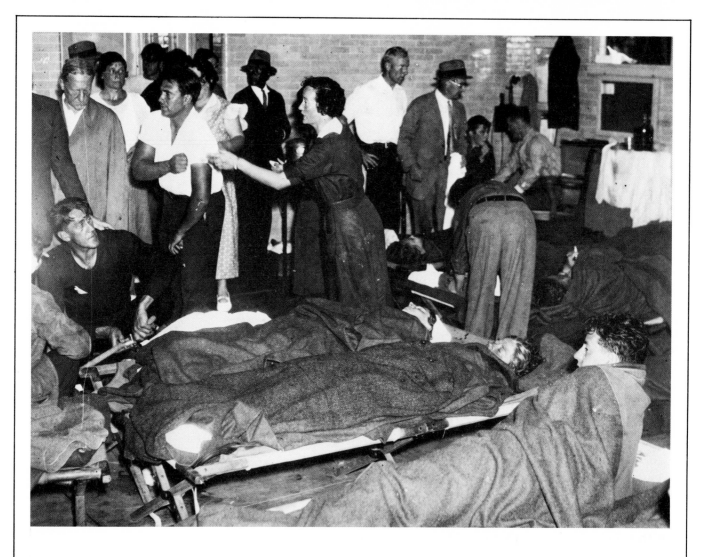

The Spring Lake, New Jersey, firehouse became a hospital to treat rescued passengers and crew members of the *Morro Castle*.

tions. First, no one thought to close the writing room's fire door and thus possibly contain the blaze. Second, when crewmen tried to get water onto the flames, they found no hose nearby—about a month before, the captain had ordered the hose removed and the fire stations capped after a woman had sprained her ankle slipping on a leaky station and had sued the ship's owners for twenty-five thousand dollars.

Unchecked, the flames raced down the corridors and through the ship. Some crewmen made inept attempts to stop the fire, but they seemed totally unprepared for the emergency. The only professional firefighter aboard was a passenger, John Kempf, of the New York City Fire Department. He tried desperately to direct sensible firefighting efforts where he was, but he soon had to flee before the inferno, along with other passengers who had mercifully awakened in time.

The abilities and judgment of the officers on the bridge seemed no better than those of the crewmen. Rather than stop the ship when the fire was first reported,

Acting Captain William F. Warms continued to plow on at twenty knots, into a wind that therefore came at the ship with a forty-knot force. The wind fanned the flames and sent them farther and farther back into the ship, trapping more and more people.

Again and again the radio operator raced to the bridge to get permission to send out an SOS, but again and again the order was not forthcoming. (In the law of the sea, an SOS gives the ships that respond to it the right to salvage fees, and perhaps, like his predecessor who removed the hose rather than risk a law suit, Captain Warms may have wanted to avoid these costs.) Finally, more than fifteen minutes after the fire was out of control, permission was given and the distress signal went out.

By this time passengers and crew were desperate. Crewmen raced for the lifeboats but had trouble getting them lowered. Passengers watched as the flames came at them, and then they could do nothing but jump into the stormy waters below, hoping that the life jackets or rings they clutched would keep them afloat until help arrived.

Daybreak found hundreds of passengers and crew, dead and alive, bobbing in the water off the New Jersey coast. A few, most of them crew members, were in *Morro Castle* lifeboats. Many others had spent the night of terror in the water. Boats from the shore and from other ships in the vicinity darted through the water, picking up the live victims first, then going back for the dead. The death toll mounted as each day more bodies washed up on shore until finally it reached 134—proportionally many more passengers than crew. As had happened so often before and would happen so often again, fire had turned a carefree dream of pleasure into a nightmare of death.

A little pleasure was all that the people who went to Boston's Cocoanut Grove nightclub on November 28, 1942, were after. The nation had been embroiled in World War II for nearly a year, so an evening out was a respite, a particular treat. And this Saturday night was a special occasion. An unusually strong Boston College football team had played Holy Cross, its traditional rival, in the afternoon. Expecting victory for their side, many Bostonians had planned victory celebrations at the Cocoanut Grove after the game. An unexpected defeat disappointed them, but hundreds went to the Grove, in the hopes of cheering themselves up. As a result, one thousand people

COCOANUT GROVE
BOSTON
1942

Firemen, priests, and servicemen watch bodies being carried from rear entrance to Cocoanut Grove nightclub, Boston, 1942.

jammed into a nightclub that was built to accommodate six hundred at most.

Actually, the nightclub had originally been built as a garage. Now it was a cavernous place divided up by plywood-covered concrete walls into a ground floor and downstairs series of cocktail lounges, dance floor, and dining rooms. The decor—fake palm trees, bamboo and rattan chairs, and billowing blue satin skies—gave the club its South Seas ambience. Leatherette walls were hardly authentic tropical design, but they were everwhere nevertheless.

At about ten o'clock on that Saturday evening, a small fire was spotted in the blue satin above a palm tree in the Melody Lounge, downstairs at the Cocoanut Grove. As it ate its way outward through the satin and on to the palm tree, waiters tried to put it out with seltzer bottles and wet bar towels. At first the guests in the lounge looked on with mild interest, but as the fire worked across the satin sky, burning bits of cloth fell on them, waking them from quiet relaxation into sudden fear. In a moment, two hundred people were running for the only exit they knew, a fairly narrow stairway leading up to the ground floor.

With that the lights went out and panic was complete. As terrified patrons struggled to mount the stairs, they heard "a hissing rush of flame over their heads." The flames flashed above them, reaching the top of the stairs faster than anyone could climb them. From there on the fire gained momentum as it made its way through the ground floor. Witnesses described it as "a great sheet of flame" that "seemed to roll in an undulating wave across the ceiling, followed immediately by volumes of thick black smoke."

Escape became more impossible by the second. Lost in the darkness and smoke, the would-be merrymakers fought to find a way out, but almost everywhere their efforts were in vain. One door to the street, at the top of the stairs from the Melody Lounge, had been welded shut —a measure the club took to ensure that no one entered or left without paying. People who went to the main entrance—a revolving door—found it jammed and the swing door next to it locked. Two other doors to the street opened inward, and, as had happened so often in other fires, the people racing to get out such doors formed a human wall sealing them shut.

The fire moved with devastating speed, the flames burning some people to death, the smoke asphyxiating others, and the nitrous oxide produced by the burning leatherette acting as an anesthetic on still others, knocking them out where they sat and leaving them to die of carbon monoxide poisoning. Within twelve minutes, everyone who would die in this disaster—492 in all—was

Tangle of chairs and tables after panic swept the burning nightclub

either dead or mortally injured. Only one hundred of the thousand Cocoanut Grove patrons escaped injury entirely.

The work that greeted Boston's firefighters as they arrived at the club was grisly indeed. Before they could reach any victims who still might be alive inside, they had to pry open heavy locked doors or dig their way through the walls of bodies that presented even more formidable barriers. At least two hundred bodies were piled against the main entrance and another hundred jammed an inward-opening exit. Then too, flames raged on, also hampering rescue work.

By 10:45, three quarters of an hour after the small spot of flame had appeared in the blue satin sky, the block-long blaze was under control. Now the sickening work of removing the charred, ruined bodies of victims could begin, and Boston's firefighters grimly set to the morbid task.

The people of Boston responded to this fire as their predecessors had after each major fire since the founding of their city in 1630. They held inquiries, assigned blame, and drew up new fire regulations to try to prevent a similar fire from ever happening again. One more time they planned against tragedy after the awesome death toll, as they had done over and over again for three hundred years.

HARTFORD CIRCUS FIRE

HARTFORD
1944

The lesson that everyone should have learned from the Cocoanut Grove disaster, and from countless fire tragedies before it, was that adequate exits must be available to enable people to get out of any enclosure within moments after danger appears. A lesson as vivid as that provided by the Cocoanut Grove should still have been fresh in every mind only a year and a half later, but events in Hartford, Connecticut, on July 6, 1944, showed that it too had been forgotten.

The day had dawned warm and damp, and it grew hotter and more humid with each passing hour. Most adults would probably have preferred to stay home with a rocker and a fan that afternoon, but children had something else in mind—the circus had just come to town and it would be leaving tomorrow.

So more than six thousand of the people of Hartford, the majority of them children, trooped off to the "Big Top," a gigantic canvas tent that stretched 425 feet by 180 feet and covered an area of one and a half acres. In a gay

144

Survivors flee the burning big top, Hartford, 1944.

mood, the crowd poured into the main entrance and filed into the rows of folding chairs and rungs of bleachers, filling the tent to three-quarters capacity. Around them they could see the thick poles that supported the tent, and high above them they could see the rope rigging and an expansive roof of heavy canvas, waterproofed with a coating of paraffin thinned with gasoline.

The show got underway with the traditional circus animal acts. Then, as the trainers were returning the lions and tigers to their cages through a series of runway chutes running down the aisles, the Flying Wallendas, a death-defying aerial act, took center ring. They had barely begun their work on the high wire when a small fire was spotted in the thin canvas wall near the main entrance. Thwarting the attempts of a circus hand to extinguish it with a few buckets of water, the fire continued up the canvas until it met the paraffin-coated roof. At this point a gust of wind picked it up and sent it racing across the "big top." Within moments the roof and the rope rigging beneath it were ablaze. As the rope burned, it released the thick support poles and sent them crashing down, carrying great chunks of the burning canvas with them.

145

ABOUT FIRE AND FIREFIGHTERS

"Firemen are going to be killed right along. They know it, every man of them ... firefighting is a hazardous occupation; it is dangerous on the face of it, tackling a burning building. The risks are plain ... Consequently, when a man becomes a fireman, his act of bravery has already been accomplished."

—New York Fire Department Chief Edward F. Croker 1908

"If Prometheus was worthy of the wrath of Heaven for kindling the first fire upon earth, how ought all the gods to honor the men who make it their professional business to put it out?"

—John Godfrey Saxe, American journalist, poet, and lecturer, circa 1850

"Fire is the best of servants; but what a master!"

—Thomas Carlyle

"A little fire is quickly trodden out, Which, being suffer'd, rivers cannot quench."

—William Shakespeare, *Henry VI,* Part III, Act IV

"Christ ain't going to be too hard On a man that died for men."

—Anonymous, "The Prairie Belle"

146

With a sea of flame above and with heavy poles and burning canvas falling to the ground around them, the audience was seized with panic. Many stampeded toward the main entrance, the way they had come in, leaving behind a tangle of collapsed folding chairs that tripped up the fleeing men, women, and children who followed. But by now the main entrance was an impassable mass of flames. Racing madly for other aisles, they found them blocked with the animal running chutes or with electrical cables. Bodies piled up as the crowd met obstruction after obstruction. Within ten minutes the entire tent fell in, burying anyone still left inside under a flaming cover.

The Hartford firefighters arrived within a few minutes of the alarm, but before they could even get into the ruin to begin rescue work, they had to soak it down to kill the remaining flames and to diminish the intense heat. They had no way of knowing what they would find inside because no one knew how many of the audience had made it to safety. At this point several of the circus performers, all of whom had escaped, were under the impression that everyone else had got out before the tent collapsed.

To their great sorrow, Hartford's firefighters found that the performers were wrong. As the rescue work went on, the firefighters unearthed victim after victim. As fast as ambulances could screech up to the smoldering tent, the rescuers loaded them with human cargo. In all 163 of the victims were dead or dying and 261 were seriously injured, many of them children, of course.

Said Emmett Kelly, the sad-faced clown who was part of the circus that day and who at first had thought that everyone had escaped, "It was the longest afternoon of my life."

Just as Emmett Kelly had faced the longest afternoon of his life on that summer day in 1944, two years later hundreds of people would face the longest night of their lives. In a brief six-month period in 1946, fire struck three hotels in the dead of night as their unsuspecting guests lay sleeping.

Shortly after midnight on June 5, a small group of people, still not ready to go off to their rooms, sat in the Silver Lounge of Chicago's LaSalle Hotel. In the twenty-one floors above them, more than a thousand people slept peacefully, in preparation for the sightseeing or business

THE LaSALLE HOTEL FIRE

CHICAGO
1946

147

Charred lobby of Chicago's LaSalle
Hotel after 1946 fire

calls or further travel that would occupy their next day.
Suddenly one of the Silver Lounge patrons leaped up
from his chair, complaining of intense heat. As he pulled
away the cushion on which he had been sitting, smoke
seeped out. A fire had been burning in the wall behind the
chair, slowly, unobstructedly, until it broke through.

Within minutes flames had enveloped the lounge
and spread out into the wood-paneled lobby. Licking its
way to the elevator shafts, the fire found easy access to
the floors above.

Hotel personnel and some guests ran through the
corridors, pounding on doors to wake the sleepers and
warn them of the danger. As the groggy hotel guests
opened their doors, they created a draft that brought
flames racing up the elevator shafts like "a pillar of fire."
Soon the entire first five floors were a roaring inferno.
Thick, noxious smoke rose to the floors above.

When the Chicago firefighters arrived, they found
hundreds of terrorized people leaning out of the hotel
windows, screaming to be saved. Some of them had fash-
ioned ropes made of sheets and were trying to escape

Guests swarm down fire escapes from LaSalle Hotel.

Firefighters and equipment in front of the LaSalle

down them. Others were throwing lamps and chairs out of the windows in a frenzied effort to get attention. Still others had climbed out onto the ledges and were poised to jump.

"Don't jump! Don't jump!" the firefighters pleaded as they raised their ladders and prepared to use their fire nets. But fear or actual flames got to many victims too soon, and they plunged down the clifflike hotel walls.

For four hours the firefighters worked desperately, putting out the flames and making their way down the dark and smoky corridors so that they could direct the uninjured to safety, rescue the injured, and remove the dead. They were able to see that nearly eight hundred guests reached safety, unharmed in body at least, and that two hundred injured were removed to hospitals. But for sixty-one guests there was nothing the firefighters could do. Death had closed in on these hapless victims with smoke and flames.

THE CANFIELD HOTEL FIRE

DUBUQUE
1946

THE WINECOFF HOTEL FIRE

ATLANTA
1946

In one of those incredible coincidences that have occasionally marked the history of American fires, within four nights of the LaSalle Hotel tragedy, a fire almost exactly parallel to it in everything but size ravaged the four-story Canfield Hotel in Dubuque, Iowa, about 165 miles away. There too, the fire was discovered in the bar, the Red Lounge in this case, shortly after midnight when most guests were sleeping. There too, flames raced through the lobby, sending blackened smoke upward to make escape difficult. And there too, the dead were counted in the morning—seventeen in all.

But it was as though these two fires were only a terrible prelude to the worst hotel fire of 1946, or of any other year in the United States.

The Winecoff Hotel, a fifteen-story structure located on Atlanta, Georgia's famous Peachtree Street, hardly seemed a likely candidate for a major fire. Built in 1913, its brick and cement construction had been considered so "fireproof" that no fire escapes were thought necessary, nor was a sprinkler system. Its proud builder, W.F. (Frank) Winecoff, was a lifetime resident of his namesake hotel.

Two guests hang out upper story window at Winecoff Hotel in Atlanta as flames leap from windows below them. Water from fire hoses streams up side of building.

NASA firemen test lightweight breathing gear at the Johnson Space Center. (NASA)

Super pumper and foam unit from New York City Fire Department.

Below: Ice-covered firefighters at work in New York City.

Opposite, clockwise from top left: Trainees practice on scaling ladders; fireboat celebrates Fourth of July with red, white, and blue streams; tower ladder directs water into upper floors of burning building; fireman carries boy down ladder as others reach to help.

(N.Y.F.D. Photo Unit)

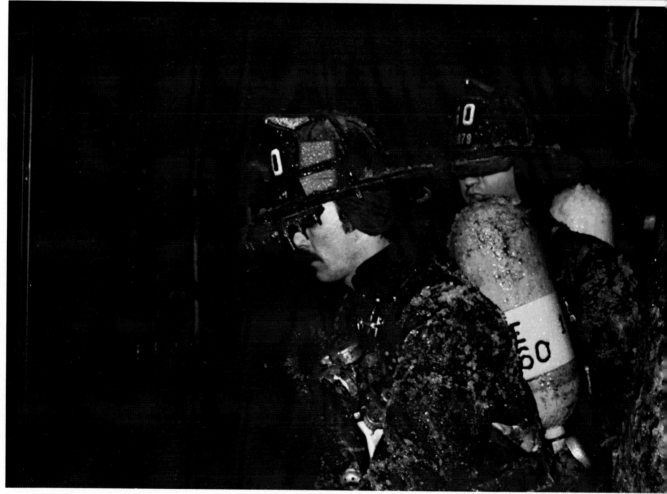

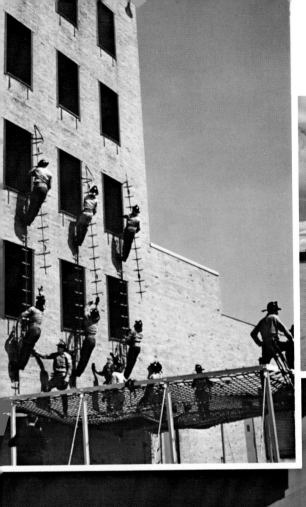

Snowflakes pattern camera lens as firefighters work on wintry fire.

Chemical foam coats scene of aircraft fire.

Firefighters use hooks on roof of New York apartment building.

(N.Y.F.D. Photo Unit)

At the height of the fire, flames burst from upper story windows of the Winecoff Hotel, 1946.

What the "fireproof" designation had not taken into consideration were the wooden baseboards, coats of paint, beds and bedding, dressers, doors, carpeting, and myriad other highly flammable furnishings within the brick and cement walls. And on the night of December 7 these all took fire, supposedly set off by a careless match dropped onto a mattress stored on the third floor.

The scene was the LaSalle Hotel all over again, but the consequence in death was even more horrific. The LaSalle at least had had fire escapes—if only people could reach them. But the guests in the Winecoff had no such chance. With the elevators soon out of commission, their only hope of escape was down an open stairway, but it soon became a path for the flames to travel, effectively cutting the panic-stricken guests off.

The Atlanta firefighters, arriving within thirty seconds of the alarm, faced the same sight that had greeted the Chicago men six months earlier—windows filled with scores of pleading figures silhouetted by the flames moving up behind them; sheets knotted into makeshift ropes dangling in the night air; bodies hurtling down, trailing screams as they went.

151

By this time the heat was so intense that flames did not even have to touch the victims to kill them—many were literally baked where they stood. Many others were asphyxiated. Twenty-five persons met their deaths as a result of mad leaps. One of these jumpers hit a firefighter carrying a woman down a ladder, sending the three of them crashing to the ground, where they all perished. The final toll was 119 dead, one of them the hotel's builder, Frank Winecoff.

THE MONSANTO FIRE

TEXAS CITY
1947

Only four months after the Winecoff fire, a disaster struck the nation that could not fail to remind witnesses of the horrors of the world war just recently ended. The scene was the Monsanto Chemical Company plant in Texas City, Texas, along the Gulf of Mexico about ten miles from Galveston; the time was eight o'clock in the morning, April 16, 1947.

Stevedores were at work loading the S.S. *Grandcamp* with a cargo of ammonium nitrate, a fertilizer bound for the war-scarred fields of Europe. At about 8:10 the workers noticed smoke coming up from the hold. After unsuccessful attempts to put the fire out, with first a jug of drinking water and then a fire extinguisher, the ship's captain ordered that steam be used to douse it. The hold was sealed and steam applied. Both the stevedores and the crew were ordered to leave the ship. Many of the stevedores, feeling that the day's work was lost, simply went home, but the crew remained at dockside, watching the action aboard.

By this time, Texas City's twenty-six-man volunteer fire company had arrived with their four pieces of equipment, and they were streaming water toward the thick orange smoke. At 9:12 the now heated and pressurized ammonium nitrate reached its exploding point. The blast that reverberated through the area was so great that it shot two planes out of the air, sending them crashing to earth. It leveled the Monsanto plant and turned concrete warehouses into crumbling ruins. It created a 15-foot tidal wave so powerful that it picked up a 150-foot steel barge and deposited it 200 feet away inland. It sent one cargo ship, the S.S. *High Flyer,* colliding into a ship across the slip, the S.S. *Wilson B. Keane,* jamming them together. It produced a fantastic rain of metal that sailed through the air with unbelievable force piercing everything in its path—glass, steel, concrete, and human flesh. (A one-ton metal drill stem shot two and a half miles through the air,

Coast Guard fireboat assists land-based firefighters during the
Monsanto Chemical Company fire in Texas City, Texas, 1947.

coming to earth with such force that it corkscrewed itself
into the ground.) And it killed at least four hundred people instantly—Monsanto employees, the stevedores and
crew who had remained near the *Grandcamp,* spectators—
and the entire Texas City volunteer fire department.

Firefighting departments and Red Cross units poured
into the area. Fire was everywhere and so was suffering
humanity. But so was heroism. With full knowledge that
they were surrounded by highly combustible fuel and
still more potentially explosive chemicals, the firefighters
and rescuers worked on.

Then, fifteen hours after the explosion, everyone was
forced to withdraw. The *High Flyer,* also carrying a cargo
of ammonium nitrate, was about to blow. At 1:10 in the
morning of April 17, the expected explosion ripped the
area. The *High Flyer* disintegrated in the blast, and the
Keane split in two, its forward half spinning end over end
onto shore. Four oil storage tanks also burst into flames,
followed in quick succession by four more.

The fires of Texas City burned on for one week with such intensity that it was impossible to determine loss of life accurately, since so many victims could have disappeared without a trace. Probably a figure of more than five hundred dead and three thousand injured and permanently maimed reflects the human damage done. Material damage was estimated at $60 million ($156.7 million today). The scene in Texas City was unprecedented in American history. Said one reporter recently returned from the war: "In four years of war coverage I have seen no concentrated devastation so utter, except Nagasaki, Japan, victim of the second atom bomb, as presented today by Texas City."

ST. ANTHONY'S HOSPITAL

EFFINGHAM, ILLINOIS
1949

The 1940s was one of the worst decades for major fires in American history. But it was as if the decade would not give up until yet another disaster marked it—this time striking one of the most pitiful of all possible scenes for a fire, a hospital.

The patients at St. Anthony's Hospital in Effingham, Illinois, had settled down for the night of April 4, 1949. Eleven of them, newly delivered mothers, knew that they would be awakened in the night for their babies' feedings, but that was a couple of hours off. In the nursery their babies slept, fussed, or quietly gurgled, watched over by nurse Fern Riley.

The other patients lay in their beds, some of them in casts or in traction, some swathed in bandages as they recovered from operations, and others weakened by disease, all trying to find a night's comfort and rest.

The hospital seemed a pleasant enough place. The Sisters of St. Francis who ran it kept it spotlessly clean. Since it was only three stories high, it did not seem so big and impersonal as many of the enormous hospitals that big-city patients had to go to. And the patients at St. Anthony's that night could also take comfort in the fact that this same hospital had served their community for nearly seventy years.

But neither the nuns' efficiency nor the hospital's long history of service could overcome the terrible fact that the hospital was a defenseless prey to fire. The brick and timber construction, the wooden floors and open wooden stairways, the combustible acoustical tile, the oilcloth-covered walls, the combustible laundry chute running from the basement to the top floor, the long,

open corridors with no barriers to fire—any one of these constituted an invitation to fire. All put together, they could create a fire both incredibly swift and totally unstoppable.

The first that anyone knew of the fire was when one of the nuns smelled smoke on the third floor. Within moments the hospital's chief engineer and Effingham's fire department were roused and on their way. Arriving first, since he lived on the grounds, the chief engineer raced down into the basement and attacked the source of the fire, in the laundry chute. Four two-and-a-half-gallon soda and acid extinguishers later, the fire roared on.

Within ten minutes, Effingham's twenty-two firefighters were on the scene, but there was little they could do other than to beg those patients who were able to drag themselves to the windows not to jump. Although there were two outside fire escapes and two slide escapes, the speed with which the fire moved cut even ambulatory patients off from them.

Rear view of St. Anthony's hospital at height of fire in Effingham, Illinois, 1949

155

OUR LADY OF THE ANGELS SCHOOL

CHICAGO
1958

Firefighters remove bodies of victims of blaze in Our Lady of the Angels elementary school in Chicago, 1958.

Firefighters responded from neighboring communities, but most of the patients—seventy-four of them—were already dead, including the eleven babies in the nursery, along with Nurse Riley, who had refused to leave them.

Perhaps nothing is so heartrending as a hospital fire unless it is another type of fire that claims the lives of the vulnerable and the helpless—a school fire. Fifty years after the dreadful Lake View Elementary School disaster that claimed 175 young lives, the nation suffered a similar tragedy—one that would call into question just how much progress had been made in fire prevention over the long span of half a century.

This time the school was in Chicago—Our Lady of the Angels Elementary School, where nearly thirteen hundred pupils were housed in a fifty-year-old building.

It was December 1958, and the school day was within a half hour of ending. Pupils began to report the smell of smoke, and before long their eyes confirmed their suspicions when smoke began to appear, seeping under the classroom doors. By this time it was estimated that the fire had been burning quietly for about thirty minutes, beginning in a rubbish heap at the foot of an open stairway.

As signs of fire began to appear, several teachers on the first floor were able to get their students out in quick and orderly fashion. But even before the school fire alarm sounded the flames flashed up the stairwell and down the long second floor corridor, trapping many pupils and teachers in their classrooms.

As in the Lake View fire, students fled to the windows, pleading to be rescued. Through the quick and heroic work of teachers and passersby, about one thousand students were brought to safety in those first terrible minutes, but that left hundreds more still inside.

Hook and Ladder Company No. 35 arrived almost immediately. Lt. Charles Kamin described the awful scene: "I ordered one ladder run up, then I ran around the corner and saw more bodies in the court and more kids at the windows. I yelled at my men to bring the other ladders and the life net to that side. I ran up one of the ladders myself. I looked around and the man behind me was being sick at his stomach. The sight was too much."

As Kamin reached the top of the ladder, another horrible sight awaited him:

> I saw the most terrifying thing in my life. In front of me was a smoke-filled window full of kids laying on top of each other in I don't know how many layers. They must have been screaming but I couldn't hear a thing. All I could think was, get them out, get them out. The ones on top of the pile were pushing so hard against the ladder I had to push them back so I could grab them one at a time by their clothes and pull them out. The heat was terrific. The kids were completely hysterical. I worked like a robot, pushing in, reaching out, dropping them down on the ground. I didn't have time to worry about the ones I dropped. If they were to live I had to get them out. I only hoped they'd fall on other children and it would break their fall. I pulled out eight—seven boys and one girl. When I pulled the eighth kid out, the air ignited and the whole window was suddenly a mass of fire. The boy's clothes caught fire but I pulled him out.
>
> Then I saw that big pile of kids, as close to me as you are, just turning dead like a burned pile of papers. . . .

By their quick work, the firefighters were able to save about 160 pupils. But for ninety-two youngsters and

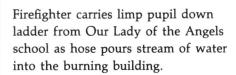
Firefighter carries limp pupil down ladder from Our Lady of the Angels school as hose pours stream of water into the burning building.

three of their teachers, there was no safety. The flames had flashed through the transoms above their classroom doors and wiped them out. Many were found still seated at their desks, some of them in prayer.

Nearly three years later another devastating fire took its toll in the soft, idyllic countryside of southern California, the kind of blaze that is every bit as fearsome as theater, hotel, or school fires. Miraculously, though, there were no lives lost, and very few injuries suffered, during the two days that out-of-control flames licked at the hills of Bel Air and Brentwood.

November 6, 1961, was an oppressively hot, dry day, and the "devil winds" that carried through Santa Ana from the Mojave Desert offered more danger than respite. Local firefighters were made anxious by the "dry level" that was the greatest in recent memory, and the Bel Air fire department sent patrol units to search for signs of smoke.

Except for the Australian interior this area consists of the most inflammable terrain in the world, abounding in high chaparral grass—oily, resinous brush, sometimes growing as high as 25 feet, that explodes as well as burns.

The dreaded fire broke out at 8:15 A.M., and within hours state, county, and federal firefighting resources were mobilized—2,500 firefighters and more than 200 pieces of fire equipment in all. Raging on, the fire fed on the natural wood shingle roofs that were the style of California architecture, lifting the burning shingles within its heat currents, and carrying them sometimes for miles, where they fell to earth to ignite whatever lay there.

Brush fires are particularly unpredictable, being governed by wind changes, and in the words of one firefighter, this fire "was treacherous and tricky, almost as if it were alive and thinking, trying to defeat us."

Finally, when the wind died, the fire was controlled, but not before it had jumped from Bel Air to Brentwood, a wealthy area populated by Hollywood stars and executives. Almost everything within a perimeter of 19 miles was burned, including 484 homes and 21 commercial buildings—a loss of more than $25 million. As in other fires where lessons were tragically learned, natural wood shingles were thereafter banned in southern California.

The Mount Hermon, Massachusetts, football team loses both the game and the school science building, 1965.

A typical scene during the riots of the 1960s: Washington, D.C., police stand guard with rifles as firemen battle flames.

FIRE AS PROTEST

WATTS
1965

With the Bel Air fire a part of history the nation began to move into an era that can be called the turbulent 1960s. Firefighters could not foretell the incredible challenges the nation's growing air of protest would present to them as the new decade literally "heated up."

First, in 1965, came Watts. There, in a black section of sprawling Los Angeles, racial anger burst into flame. On August 11, a minor incident involving a white policeman arresting a black motorist for driving while intoxicated set off several days of uncontrollable rioting.

Early on in the brick-throwing, car-overturning melee, the rioters turned to fire as a weapon. Homes, stores, public buildings—nothing was safe from the torch. And no firefighter who came into the area to quench the blazes was safe from taunts, rocks, sniper fire, and Molotov cocktails. At least four firefighters were shot as they tried to do their work and one was killed by a falling wall, a victim of the mindless arson that swept the area. Even National Guardsmen riding atop the fire equipment could not protect it—more than 100 pieces were damaged—nor could they protect the firefighters. Nearly two hundred of them were injured.

When the fires finally died away and the anger subsided, thirty-four people lay dead and more than a thousand lay injured amid millions of dollars' worth of damage. The nation could hope that the Watts riots were just a temporary aberration—a self-inflicted tragedy so great that it would never be repeated. The nation could hope, but time and again it would be sadly disappointed.

In the next few years city after city underwent a similar fate as racial tensions grew rather than diminished. Newark, New Jersey in 1967. New York and Detroit in the same year. Then in 1968 the assassination of Martin Luther King sparked another outbreak of arsonous rioting. Great areas of Chicago and Washington, D.C. took on the look of war zones, and again the firefighters who tried to save lives and property were attacked and thwarted. Indeed, to the rioters, it was the firefighters who seemed to be the enemy. Thus, during the 1960s, the most dangerous occupation in the nation—firefighting—became more dangerous still.

As rioters emerged as new foes of firefighters, the old foes—heat, smoke, falling walls, collapsing floors, vast concentrations of highly flammable substances, to name just a few—continued to be just as formidable as ever, a fact of life made all too clear to the men of New York City's fire department on October 17–18, 1966.

Fire had broken out in a Twenty-third street drugstore in a commercial area of the city, and soon it had worked its way down a row of stores in three buildings. Four fire companies raced to the scene—Engine Nos. 5 and 18 and Ladder Nos. 2 and 7. Soon two groups of men entered the building where the fire had started—about half a dozen going into the cellar and another dozen moving into the main floor. Within minutes the cellar had become an inferno.

"Get out, get out," came the cry, and the men in the cellar rushed out. Then with a thunderous crash, a twenty-by-five-foot section of the main floor gave way, plunging ten of the men there to certain death in the fiery hole below. The flames that came gushing out of the newly opened floor trapped another two men and claimed their lives as well.

THE 23rd STREET FIRE

NEW YORK
1966

161

Firefighters bow their heads as one of their comrades is carried from the ruins of the 1966 New York fire that claimed the lives of twelve firemen.

GULF OIL REFINERY FIRE

PHILADELPHIA
1975

Said one man from Engine No. 18 who had been working outside the building, "I went over and shouted inside, 'Eighteen! Eighteen!' But there was nobody to answer me."

In a few moments' time, twelve brave firefighters had lost their lives, including one rookie whose first—and last—fire it was. The Chief of the Department lamented, "This was the saddest day in the 100-year history of the Fire Department. I know we all died a little."

Nine years later, Philadelphia's firefighting force must have felt that they too had "died a little." On August 17, 1975, flames came to life in what surely must be among the most dreaded and most dangerous scenes for a fire—an oil refinery.

Shortly after midnight the tanker *Afran Neptune*, docked in Philadelphia's Schuylkill River, had begun to pump its cargo of crude oil into Gulf Oil Company's Tank 231, capacity seventy-three thousand barrels. Within a few hours the tank was overfilling, the result of carelessness in monitoring the amount going in. Soon trapped hydrocarbon vapors began seeping out under the tank's floating roof, seeking something to fire them. At about 6:00 A.M. they found it at a nearby boiler house and then flashed back into the tank. Soon burning oil was overflowing the vents and washing down the tank.

Six alarms in the first forty-eight minutes brought two hundred Philadelphia firefighters, who set to work

Flames and smoke billow around Gulf Oil tanks in Philadelphia.

Firemen battle crude oil blaze at Gulf Oil Refinery in Philadelphia, 1975, where eight firefighters were killed in the line of duty.

High-pressure monitor delivers deluge from the deck of a fireboat at Brooklyn pier fire.

with cooling hose and foam to bring the blaze under control. Another five alarms brought additional firefighters.

At about three o'clock in the afternoon an electrical failure caused two of the pumps that were draining away the foam and water runoff to shut down. As firefighters slogged through the growing level of runoff, they did not know that hydrocarbon seepage had joined with it, making it highly flammable.

At 4:40 the inevitable happened. The overflow flashed, setting three firefighters who were walking through it afire. Five of their comrades, safely on higher ground but seeing their plight, rushed down to help them. But it was no use. Not only were the three men initially caught in the flames killed, but so were three of the men who tried to save them. Later the bodies of two more firefighters were also found nearby, bringing to eight men the loss to Philadelphia's firefighting force that horrible Sunday.

Firefighting has always been a dangerous calling, but there have been technological advances to help and to protect the firefighter in his age-old combat. A super pumper capable of delivering 8,800 gallons of water per minute from a source of water over a mile away has been developed, and is now in use in New York City. Snorkels and Tower Ladders are now in operation in many towns and cities—apparatus that permit the firefighter, riding in a bucket, to rise up the outside of a building a distance of nine stories from the ground. Indeed, the city of Chicago has a 150-foot Morita ladder that rises fifteen stories.

After the tragic 1967 spaceship fire at Cape Kennedy in which three astronauts perished, the National Aeronautics and Space Administration became involved in fire research, and those efforts have produced a flameproof, lightweight material to replace the heavy, meltable, and flammable rubber coats that firefighters normally wear. American industry has also given much attention in recent years to fire research, and has provided safer and more durable helmets, boots, gloves, air masks, hose and nozzles.

Despite advances in equipment, it cannot be said that live firefighters are well protected. For all the technological innovations, firefighting is still the nation's most hazardous occupation, and America still suffers more fire losses, in lives and in economic costs, than any other country in the world.

While we have had serious fires in high-rise buildings, we have thus far been spared the catastrophic fatalities in high-rises that occurred in Brazil, Korea, and Ger-

Firefighters climb ladder to floors above a burning restaurant in New York.

Ninety-five-foot tower ladder carries firefighters from street to rooftop fire.

"Knocking down" a fire in a cockloft (the space between ceiling and roof). Modern tower ladder gives great, and safe, mobility.

many. Building codes in America are left to the jurisdiction of local governments, and consequently buildings that are essentially unsafe are still being built in many parts of the country—buildings without sprinkler systems, buildings with heat-touch elevator buttons that bring elevators automatically to the hazards of the fire floor, buildings with uncontrolled duct systems that allow smoke and heat to travel freely from floor to floor, buildings with elevators that cannot be controlled by firefighters on the main floor, and buildings in which fireproof emergency stairwells can possibly act as flues in which anyone attempting to use them can be consumed. The possibility still exists of one high-rise fire taking as many lives as the Great Chicago Fire, or even the Peshtigo Conflagration.

The lessons of tragic fires have not been fully appreciated, and buildings of public gathering still exist without adequate means of escape, without smoke and fire alarms, and without sprinkler systems.

The horror of Boston's Cocoanut Grove fire was repeated on a clear spring night, May 28, 1977, in Southgate, Kentucky. More than three thousand people were gathered in the Beverly Hills Supper Club, one of the largest night clubs in the country, to hear the entertainer

BEVERLY HILLS SUPPER CLUB

SOUTHGATE, KENTUCKY
1977

Men and equipment battle Kentucky supper club blaze, 1977.

John Davidson sing. A fire began in the electrical wiring in the wall space of the Zebra Room, one of the club's many banquet rooms, and several of the club's employees tried to locate and then extinguish the flames. The alarm to the Fire Department was delayed for over fifteen minutes, and the fire began to spread. A busboy, Walter Bailey, eighteen, realized the danger and jumped to the stage, interrupting a comedy act. Coolly, he told the audience that there was a fire in the building, and he pointed to the exits of the room, but the people thought he was part of the comedy act, and remained in their seats for a few fateful minutes. There were no smoke alarms in the building, no sprinkler system. Suddenly thick, black smoke began to push down from the air conditioning ducts. The lights went out. There was no clear means of egress from the building, but a series of corridors and foyers. Confused and disoriented, the people panicked. When the fire was finally extinguished there were 165 dead.

Fire losses in America have been so great that Congress has set up the National Fire Prevention and Control Administration. Mandated by law in 1975, the NFPCA gives a national focus and authority to what has traditionally been a local problem, and will undoubtedly go far in reducing needless life and property losses due to fire. It is yet a young agency and time alone will determine the

Firefighters' courage takes many forms:

Chicago firemen wrestle a ruptured hose (above);

ice and snow hamper New York City firefighters (opposite and overleaf).

federal government's effectiveness in meeting the challenge of the national fire problem.

Firefighting and the history of fire in America are, peculiarly, at once both romantic and deadly. Firefighting itself is exciting and glamorous. The ring of the sirens, the flashing of the lights, the leaping of the flames, and the possibility of courage—those heroic actions that make men stand apart from the crowd—engender in the imagination the spirit and passion from which myths are created. Romantics caught in a pragmatic world, the nation's firefighters are the last of a breed of great American adventurers. The motivation for working, for living, is fundamental and uncomplicated—good versus evil, preservation versus destruction, and life versus death. It is all quite innocent. There is a fire that must be extinguished, for all fires are ultimately extinguished, and the firefighter knows that few can do as he does. The goal is clear, the reward immediate. The firefighter works as one of a team, yet he seems always quite alone in a building that is burning. The present is always tenuous, the future always in question.

The world might be pragmatic, but the firefighter lives in an idealized world where men serve others at the risk of their own lives, a red whirl of a world in which men feel good about themselves and about their work. There is an enviable independence that grows from this ability to square off daily against danger, to give death a tickle behind the ear every now and again.

Yet, for all of that, there is a dark and brutal dimension to firefighting. The firefighter goes into a burning building to search for anyone who might not have made it out, to locate the fire, and to extinguish it. But the area surrounding a fire is untenable for all but those who have trained themselves to operate in a hostile environment where their bodies are being assaulted. Smoke and heat, being lighter than air, rise to the ceiling and then bank down. The firefighter crawls, nose to the floor, the heat attacking his face and sinking deeply into all pores until it seems that the skin drips. Often, he has not had time to harness an air canister to his back to give him the protection of a mask, and the smoke enters his lungs and works its way through the bloodstream to the brain. Smoke does nothing for longevity. The body reacts, and viscous black stuff flows from the nose and mouth, mixes with a stream of perspiration, and falls to the floor. There is much coughing and choking, perhaps vomiting. All

Rescues are a normal part of
firefighters' work, but never
become routine: long climbs
down ladders, mouth-to-mouth
resuscitation, digging out a
man trapped in a construction cave-in.

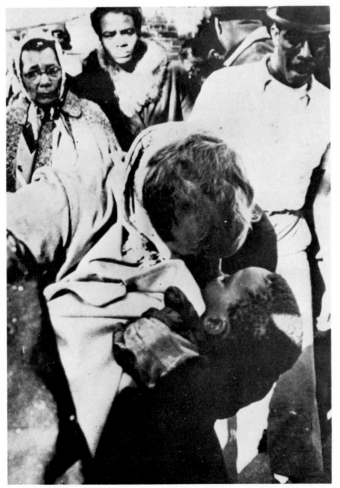

energy is being used, and there is weakness, a strange sense of semiconsciousness. The flames are met, and fought. The price of the adventure is paid.

More firefighters are killed in the performance of duty than are the members of any other occupation—more than miners, construction workers, and police officers. The severity rate of injuries among firefighters is the highest in the country.

Firefighting is tough, dirty work, but firefighters accept the brutality of their calling as we accept the storms of winter.

The history of great fires is filled with stories of valor in firefighting, but it is also filled with stories of great personal tragedies. Most fires recounted in this book have a loss figure that is calculated in dollars, but how can we calculate the cost in human suffering—the charred loves, the smoldering dreams?

Firefighters show their concern as they rush a limp fire victim from her house.

A volunteer rescues a pet kitten.

Firefighter tenderly warms a wet, chilled child inside his coat.

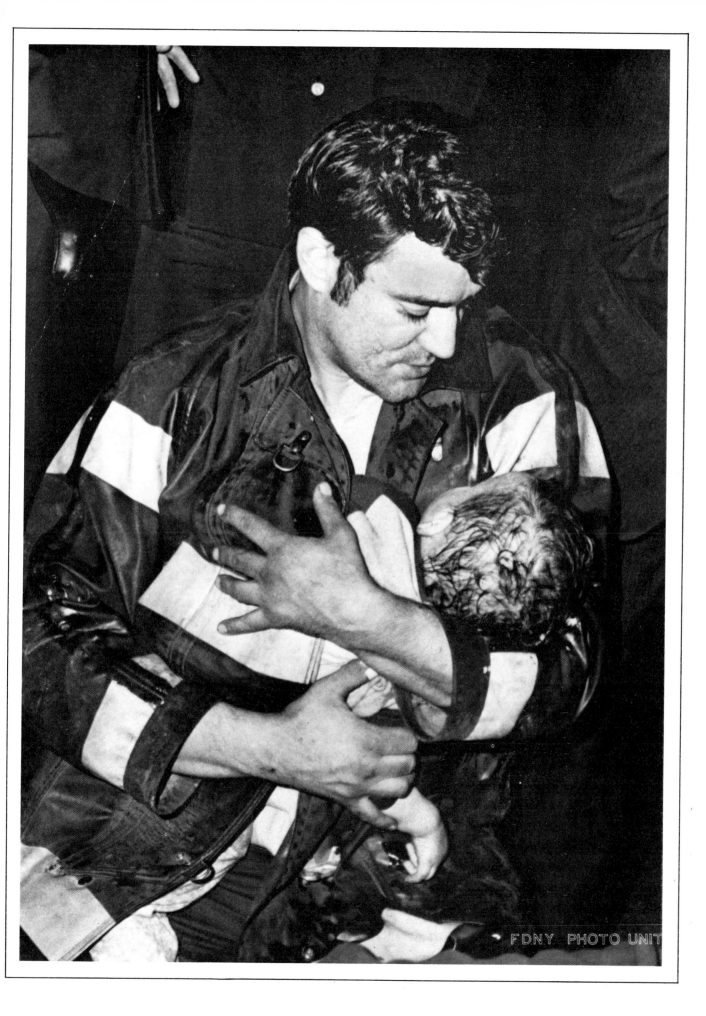

FDNY PHOTO UNIT

INDEX

(Numbers in italics refer to illustrations.)